Reflective Thinking and Professional Development

Reflective Thinking and Professional Development: A Primer

KELVIN L. SEIFERT

THE UNIVERSITY OF MANITOBA

HOUGHTON MIFFLIN COMPANY   BOSTON   NEW YORK

Senior sponsoring editor: Loretta Wolozin
Associate editor: Lisa Mafrici
Senior project editor: Rosemary Winfield
Production/design coordinator: Jodi O'Rourke
Senior manufacturing coordinator: Sally Culler

Printed in the U.S.A.

ISBN: 0-395-96449-0

1 2 3 4 5 6 7 8 9-QF-02 01 00 99 98

C O N T E N T S

2

Thinking About Thinking

3

$\mathcal{H}$earing Distant Voices: Interpreting Teacher Research

4

$\mathcal{L}$ooking Ahead: Developing as a Professional

INTRODUCTION TO THIS PRIMER

This primer is a response to a concern among teachers that is both old and new—the drive (and desire) to develop teaching further as a profession. Throughout the two or three centuries history of public education, "professionalism" has lingered as an issue. The language in which the issue is expressed has evolved and shifted over time. In earlier decades the path to professionalism was often expressed in terms of teachers' need for university degrees or additional university credits. More recently, it has been expressed in terms of a need for national professional teaching standards (like the ones discussed in Chapter 4 of this primer).

But the essential concerns behind these proposals have remained unchanged. In essence, teachers and society have both continually wondered how we teachers can relate helpfully, fairly, and effectively to other people's children. How can we teach students so they not only learn but learn well? How can we teach them so they want to learn—so they feel motivated, rather than forced? How can we teach them so that we honor the many differences among them?

Many of the proposals for dealing with these questions have had considerable merit, especially when the context of the proposals is taken into account. It is my belief, however, that a key element in developing teachers' professionalism lies less with the specifics of particular proposals for reform and more with teachers themselves. To be truly professional, teachers must develop their own beliefs and knowledge about what it means for teaching—and learning—to be "good." Given the nature of education, teachers' beliefs and knowledge will inevitably take account of ideas and recommendations from numerous individuals inside and outside the classroom. But in the end, all ideas must be constructed and "owned" by classroom teachers themselves. There is no other pathway to professionalism in education.

This belief—that teachers must construct their own path to professionalism—has guided me in writing this primer, *Reflective Thinking and Professional Development*. Its four chapters grew out of a longer book, *Constructing a Psychology of Teaching and Learning*, which deals not only with issues of professionalism but also with a number of other topics related to the foundations of teaching and learning. The issue of professionalism is so broad and so relevant to diverse areas of education, however, that it deserves a separate discussion, like the one offered here. This primer is intended not only for education students taking foundations or educational psychology courses, but also for many others—students in methods courses, for example, or future teachers currently undertaking practice teaching, or current teachers taking stock of their work and of their relationship to teaching as a career.

Whatever your current status or situation, the primer invites you to reflect on your relationship to teaching, and on how you want to develop it. Chapter 1 focuses especially on what you already have to offer students—knowledge about teaching you have gained from experience or other prior study. Chapter 2 looks at the diversity of ways that students learn—the many ways in which they think—and at the challenges that the diversity presents to you as a teacher. Chapter 3 explores how you (and teachers in general) can create knowledge for yourself about teaching and learning, through making use of teachers' own explorations of their work and even through undertaking your own explorations as "action" researchers. Chapter 4 discusses how your knowledge and experience, both prior and current, can point you in useful—and increasingly professional—directions in the future.

In all four chapters, the focus continually returns to you: to what you know and believe about teaching and learning and to how you want to revise your own knowledge and beliefs. For this purpose I use some techniques originated in this primer's "parent" book, *Constructing a Psychology of Teaching and Learning*. In each chapter, for example, I frequently invite you to consider significant questions in boxes called "In Your Own Voice." The questions are all related to the topics of the chapter and of some significance to classroom teaching and learning. Most important, they call for answers that only you can give: in most cases they lack any single "right" answers.

In each chapter, as well, there is a boxed comment called "Multiple Voices" from a teacher or educational researcher about some aspect or point within the chapter. As you will see, their comments not only add to the ideas that I present but occasionally also imply disagreement with mine. Just as with my direct questions to you as readers, therefore, the "Multiple Voices" boxes illustrate a key of this primer and of teaching in general—that it takes many voices to create the field of education.

I invite you to become one of those voices. Use this book as a place to begin thinking and discussing what it means to teach, and add your ideas to the ones printed here.

Kelvin Seifert

Reflective Thinking and Professional Development

CHAPTER VIEW

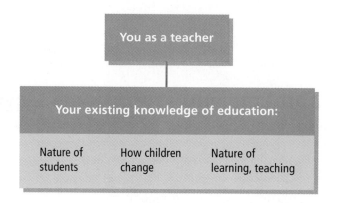

Chapter View: Starting with Your Experience and Knowledge   This Chapter View is a concept map that indicates one among many ways of thinking about the chapter. It suggests a starting point, conceptually, for the chapter but is incomplete by itself. At the end of the chapter is a Chapter Re-View, which expands on the Chapter View, suggesting directions for taking your thinking further—though, of course, other directions are also possible.

1

Starting with Your Experience and Knowledge

This primer revolves around two ideas, **teaching** and **learning**. It assumes you already know something about both and have experienced them in countless ways. You have witnessed teaching in classrooms, at home, and among your friends. You may have even done some teaching yourself. And you have experienced learning virtually every day, not only in the classroom but also during informal conversations with peers or when reading a book or watching a good television show. Your experiences with teaching and learning are unique to you; no one else has learned exactly what you have learned or seen what you have seen. In the course of these experiences, furthermore, you have already formed beliefs and views about the nature of the processes themselves: observations, impressions, and inferences about how teaching occurs or learning is experienced in general. Unless you have been a teacher, you may not have reflected much on your ideas; but it is impossible not to have them, given how experiences with teaching and learning pervade our society.

This primer also assumes you are open to new ideas about what it means to teach and to learn, and willing to look at perspectives that have not been part of your experience until now. I will invite you to consider what you believe about teaching and learning in relation to ideas held by others—ideas expressed both in published writings and in informal conversations with peers. This task will be challenging because it will mean questioning beliefs you may have held for a long time. Some of your ideas, even your most cherished ones, may turn out to be less reasonable than you first supposed.

In the pages ahead, I will invite you to recognize your ideas alongside those offered here, even if (or perhaps especially if) they seem concrete or "local" in relevance. At the same time, I will urge you to recognize the value of systematic inquiry about teaching and learning. I will also call attention to the social quality of learning as you and other students and teachers actually experience it. In the classroom, for example, teacher and student talk to each other, write and make assignments for each other, and influence each other's actions in numerous ways, all in the interest of promoting learning. Among these social experiences are some that look solitary, such as when a student reads a book or writes an essay. But the "independence" of these actions is more apparent than real: always the book has been written and assigned by other people, always the essay ideas are based on dialogues with other human beings.

Instead of calling this publication a short text or book, you might better think of it as a dialogue or conversation about teaching and learning, with you participating in that dialogue. It is guided by a specific but very broad philosophical perspective called **constructivism**, a belief that knowledge is created or "constructed" by active efforts to make meaning and by individuals' interactions with other people and with things in order to do so. You will see this term, and variants of it, frequently in all four chapters, though most of the time you will simply see ideas that imply or point toward constructivism. Various ideas about teaching and learning will be described, as well as assorted experiences undergone by students and teachers. These will invite you to think and to talk: to interpret my descriptions with ideas and experiences of your own. The book will present one "truth" about education but a number of truths. Your own, personally evolving truth about teaching and learning can form alongside these others, and partially in response to them.

How do you suppose first impressions will alter later experiences that these three people will form of each other? Will they reflect on their impressions in ways that will alter their opinions?
© Michael Newman/PhotoEdit

Experience: Pitfalls and Potentials

In Your Own Voice

Think about how your own experience may have misled you—for example, when your first impression of someone was mistaken.

What made you change your mind about the person later?

Of course, you may have had further experiences with the person, but think carefully: did the additional experiences also make you reflect or reinterpret your earlier impressions?

As you become more involved in teaching, you may hear much about the value of personal experience. Experience is the best teacher, it is said: your encounters with students should show you how to teach effectively. We have all attended public school classrooms, for example, so this universal experience should help ready us to teach more than other, more deliberate experiences further removed from classrooms, such as reading books or attending discussions about teaching.

The trouble with this commonsense idea is that it assumes what you take or learn from experience will be obvious. Suppose I have indeed experienced many classrooms and teachers in my lifetime, but the classrooms varied widely in quality: some were good and some were very bad. If I am to benefit from this motley assortment of experiences, something must tell me how to sort the good from the bad—how to tell a good teacher from a bad one, or a helpful classroom practice from one that wastes time or even is harmful. At the extremes, intuition may indeed make this possible. We can all tell the difference (we hope) between a fabulous teacher and a horrible one. But many—perhaps most—experiences with education are not extreme, and sorting out their effects therefore takes thought. Was it good or bad that one of my former teachers assigned classroom tests; was it motivating or intimidating? Was it good or bad that another one worked a lot with individuals, or did this actually mean the majority often got neglected?

These questions have more than one response. If you do not agree with me that they do, try answering them yourself, trying deliberately to consider more than one point of view about them. Is there *always* a clear-cut answer about the effects of testing or about how much time to spend with individuals? If you still think these questions have unambiguous answers, try discussing them with two or three friends. Chances are that at some point in your lives, each of you has experienced classroom tests and teachers who sometimes worked with individuals. Do you all have the same viewpoint about the educational effects of these experiences?

As it is with notions of *teaching,* so it is with notions of *learning:* experience does not lead to uniform, predictable understandings of "what" learning is. Both you and your friend may have learned Spanish from elementary school onward, but you learned it entirely at school whereas your friend learned it partly from her family at home. Your ideas of what it means to "teach and learn Spanish" may therefore differ dramatically, even if you have achieved similar proficiency with the language. Experience has mattered, but mattered in different ways. If the two of you say—or anyone else says—that "we learned from experience," you will have to say what you mean by that idea.

Reflection: Partner of Experience

*W*HY is experience such an ambiguous teacher? One factor is probably the sheer diversity of human experience. But this is only part of the story. Another factor is the diversity of human **reflection** on experience, or how we consider, ponder, or tax our minds about topics and experiences. Everyone thinks about or interprets what happens in individual ways, and before you know it, we develop individual interpretations about events, interpretations that act as guides for further experiences and reflections (Russell & Munby, 1991; Schön, 1991). In school, the scenario might look like this: two of your friends take the same course from the same instructor, but their assessments of the course differ because they think about or reflect on the experience differently. As John thinks about the course, he sees different meanings in the experience (getting a good grade, finding a job) than Sara sees (learning new material, listening to an interesting professor). Their separate views grow out of separate reflections on experience. The stage is set for further differences to develop between John and Sara: for distinct interpretations of subsequent courses and for distinct choices of later courses. Eventually their thinking about learning may be more different than similar, and reaching common understandings about education may require still further reflections on both their parts.

The Results of Reflection: Celebrating Uniqueness

*I*T seems, then, that experience and reflection lead each of us to construct somewhat unique meanings for *teaching* and *learning*. The diversity of these ideas is pervasive. It occurs in teachers' lounges in schools and at professional conferences on education. The diversity can lead to disconcerting misunderstandings. Consider the following two teachers, who work in a single school building. Jan and Frank differ in crucial ways. Yet both do something they call "teaching," and both encourage something they call "learning."

How different can two colleagues be? Jan Collins and Frank Burstow teach fifth grade in the same elementary school—in adjacent rooms, as a matter of

There are many ways to develop shared understandings, and not all of them require continuous conversation. These students may arrive at a common understanding of their experiment even though each is making a unique contribution to it.
© Gale Zucker/Stock Boston

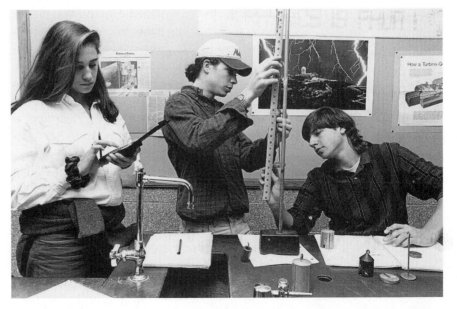

fact. Jan uses a lot of self-chosen projects for her students, like the one three kids are doing now to "find out everything we can about space travel." She has her students keep journals about their projects and other activities, and reads to them without fail every week, or even more. She also keeps a journal for herself, in which she reflects on experiences and impressions about the students and daily activities.

When I visited Jan's room, she showed me her journal, now in its third binder even though it was only January. Her latest entries contained detailed personality sketches of each of the twenty-five children, collectively entitled "What I Know Now About My Students." She had gathered impressions from individual conversations she had had as well as from students' work and from informal conversations with parents and other staff. She could not talk with me during the lunch hour because of a teachers' meeting: "Several of us have lunch every few weeks to talk about the kids in each other's classes."

Next door, Frank prides himself in knowing his students. For him this means giving them frequent tests in all subjects and supporting the school district's program of standardized testing. He knows nearly all of his students' test scores by heart and keeps careful records of both their standardized and classroom-based scores, which he proudly showed me. The scores, he feels, are a prime indicator of what his students are learning, and help him to plan each week's instruction. The day I visited, Frank gave a vocabulary lesson: the kids read printed excerpts using difficult words, then took a practice test asking them to define each word. The test was multiple-choice. In fact, the test sheet looked a lot like a page from one of the standardized language tests; Frank had even printed his practice test using the same typeface used for the standardized test. Most students did well on it, though some had to take a retest on words they missed initially.

After school, I sat down with Jan and Frank to thank them for letting me to visit their rooms and express my appreciation for their work.

"One thing about this school," said Jan, "is that the teachers really know their students and *take students' learning into account*." Frank nodded in agreement.

The gap that I had seen still fresh in my mind, I asked, "Tell me more about that. What do you mean by 'taking learning into account'?" I looked hopefully at both of them, ready for a long discussion.

As you can imagine, this question prompted very different responses from these two teachers, and I did not leave the school very soon.

If you were a mutual colleague of Jan and Frank, how would you have dealt with the differences between them? It will not do simply to ignore one person's views about *teaching* and *learning* and listen to another's; this strategy not only risks offending a colleague but also keeps you from learning from that colleague. Neither will it do simply to adopt one teacher's ideas about *teaching* and *learning* uncritically and completely. Chances are the ideas will be based on experiences somewhat different from yours, and therefore will neither fit your past nor support your future adequately. Your only option will be to develop your own personal perspective on *teaching* and *learning*, one tailored to your own particular experiences and goals. Ideas from others can help you do this, of course, but ultimately you will have to form your own opinions, claim ownership of your unique perspective, and be ready to explain yourself to teachers and parents who may disagree with you. Learning to do this in a way that maintains mutual respect between you and others can be a challenge, but it can be done. This book is meant to help you meet that challenge by stimulating your thinking and dialogue about the issues involved in *teaching* and *learning*.

Constructing *Teaching* and *Learning* Through Dialogue

*D*IALOGUE is indeed a key to dealing with differences in viewpoints about teaching and learning. Dialogue is valuable whether you are a student, a new teacher, or a veteran teacher.

Two students commenting about what makes a teacher good:

"She listens to me; doesn't just boss."

"When he talks to you, it sounds like he heard what you said, like it mattered. Like maybe I even changed his thinking a little."

Two first-year teachers commenting on why they like the school where they work:

"The old-timers take your comments seriously. It seems like they want to hear from me about my classes, even though they've seen it all before."

"The teacher in the room next door has taught for twenty years, and she gives me lots of good ideas for my kids. But she doesn't insist that I use them or insist that I agree with her."

Two veteran teachers commenting on why they have had a good year:

"The kids behaved OK this year, but they also had spunk. They really were willing to talk about things, like they were thinking for themselves."

"Those two new teachers at our building, they weren't afraid to talk about their classes. It makes conversation easier. I wasn't afraid of them being overawed, of always agreeing with me just to be nice."

Dialogue! What a wonderful way to begin a book that deals with teaching and learning! After all, the work of the teacher is primarily oral dialogue. The teacher has educative conversations with students, other teachers and educational professionals, parents, friends and family members, himself/herself, and texts. So it really makes sense to think about dialogue as being important also in learning to teach.

What I like about the particular approach taken is that Kelvin believes that both formal and informal dialogue are important in the learning process. Informal dialogue that goes on in an individual's head is intriguing to me, although I certainly acknowledge and have conducted research on the importance of formal dialogue in learning to teach. Informal/internal dialogue includes our conversations with texts, with ourselves in trying to figure out what just happened, and with others who are not present.

A very big piece of the current literature on teaching relates to reflection; and reflection may be considered as conversation with oneself. In fact, one of the most intriguing forms of reflection was called by Donald Schön [a professor at the Massachusetts Institute of Technology] *reflection-in-action*. This happens when the class is moving right along and something may jar the flow: a dilemma may crop up, or a quite unexpected student response may take place. At this point, the teacher may begin to have a dialogue with the classroom "action"—a reflection-in-action. What is going on? Why? What should I do now? These are important dialogues since they help us with next steps, and also provide learning experiences that allow us to avoid pitfalls next time.

Virginia Richardson, University of Michigan

Not only teachers and students but also observers of education agree on the value of thoughtful conversation, dialogue, and other forms of give-and-take about educational issues. That is essentially what Virginia Richardson, professor of teacher education at the University of Michigan, is saying in the accompanying Multiple Voices box: be thoughtful, but be sure to share your thoughtfulness.

Dialogue in Person

These comments suggest that a good response to the differences among educators lies in **dialogue,** the active sharing of views intended to clarify differences and identify common ground. Dialogue takes many forms, from short exchanges to long conversations, and it can involve many people or just a few. It can even include people whom you never see, such as the author of a book or a media personality: sometimes you "talk" with such a person in your mind as though she or he were sitting in the same room. Whatever its form, dialogue is marked by mutual respect among the participants, even when they do not agree on particular points. Its goal is common understanding, though not necessarily full agreement. For complex matters such as teaching and learning, dialogue often can continue for long periods, and may in fact never finish: you never really decide what teaching or learning is, once and for all. This does not mean you have to talk day and night for months to understand education. It means only that conversations about these things will never really end; they will just be interrupted periodically so that you and your conversational partners can eat, sleep, or teach the next day of school. Sooner or later, the dialogue begins again—and again.

Dialogue with Text

All this may seem plausible enough for conversations with your immediate community: your friends or your current teachers. But you may be less convinced that dialogue is possible with the unseen members of your educational community, such as the author of a textbook or a renowned authority on education. If a textbook author (myself, for example) asserts something in print with which you do not immediately agree, can you really do anything other than just accept the idea as authoritative? Even here, dialogue is possible and helpful. You can, of course, discuss an author's ideas with classmates or instructors. But you can also "talk" to the author in spirit, if not in fact. You can hold a sort of mental conversation between the author and yourself, as Jodi does in the following example. Jodi has never met the person who wrote the text she is reading, but she considers the author's ideas just as actively as she would if the author were in the same room with her. You may also sense a bit of skepticism in Jodi at times, a questioning that actually helps her come to terms with what she reads.

Jodi was reading her textbook in educational psychology, thinking and taking notes as she went along.

Conservation is the belief in or perception of constancy or invariance despite visible changes.

"Huh? Jargon again; I wish this author would speak more plainly." Jodi highlighted the word conservation with a bright pink felt-tip pen ("Sounds important," she thought).

Consider two glasses of water of the same size and shape. If a young preoperational child looks at these, he will have no trouble agreeing that they contain the same amount of water.

She highlighted the word preoperational. She remembered the prof using this term during discussion last week. "Little kids—preschoolers?" Jodi paused over the words trouble agreeing . . .

But if one of the glasses is poured into a wide, low jar, he may decide that it now has "less" water.

. . . and then over the word decide. "Sounds like a committee meeting—like the kid is discussing his thoughts with the water."

The lower height stands out perceptually and appears to distract him from noticing that it is compensated for by greater width. Older, concrete operational children are not distracted in this way. For them the amount of water in each glass stays the same regardless of how its shape changes.

Jodi wrote in her notes: "Conservation depends on paying attention." But then she crossed it out.

"No, that can't be what they mean by 'distraction.' Everyone gets distracted sometimes." She remembered a heated debate with a friend at a neighborhood hangout when the bartender brought "identical" drinks in different-shaped glasses. She was sure she received less for her money! Conservation might be something that even she lacked, not just little kids. Finally, she just wrote in her notes, "Ask Prof what they mean by 'getting distracted.'"

In theoretical terms, they "conserve" the amount of water in their minds in spite of visible changes that suggest an alteration.

Jodi heaved a sigh and closed her book, then looked again at her notes. "Who is 'they'?" she wondered. Was it really *all* older children or just a majority or just the ones who have been studied?

How Many Voices Create the Psychology of Teaching and Learning?

OR various reasons, it can be tempting to accept an author's voice automatically in preference to your own; after all, whatever is in print should represent careful thought, if not "the" truth.

Published authors do have the advantage of time to reflect on what they write—in this case, to reflect on teaching and learning. Presumably they have also done a lot of talking about educational issues. In textbooks, in particular, authors try to summarize "the state of the field," meaning they try to speak on behalf of educators as a whole. In a sense, therefore, other educators are also talking whenever "the" author speaks, and when you read a text, you will actually "hear" many voices, not just one.

These are important reasons to take published perspectives on teaching and learning seriously, but they are still not good enough to justify accepting an author's perspective without question. No matter how many experts have discussed it, any particular theory of teaching or learning will not necessarily be appropriate or useful for your goals, values, or activities. Some theories may make assumptions that can seem wrong-headed. One may assume, for example, that learning is like the activities of a computer. Thinking of student learning in this way may be helpful in planning your classes—and then again, it may not. Even if you are skeptical of the computer metaphor, though, it is important to understand it as well as you can so that you can also understand *why* you object to it. Striking a balance between belief and skepticism can be difficult, but in the end it is productive: you will end up with a deeper understanding of both teaching and learning and of both your own thinking and that of the published authors.

Even when we have the "same" experience, we may react to it differently. In the classroom, providing common experiences is no guarantee of common outcomes.
© Helen Nestor/Monkmeyer

Publications about teaching and learning thus merit your consideration; but so do your own ideas (Bereiter, 1994; Fenstermacher, 1994). To formulate your own perspective, then, you will have to "negotiate" your interpretations of *teaching* and *learning* with others' interpretations; that is, you will have to compare your ideas with the ones you read about as well as with those you hear about. The negotiation is in effect an internal, constructive dialogue, one that respects both your beliefs about teaching and learning and the theoretical perspectives described later in this book.

To summarize: dialogue can be either outward conversation or inward thoughtfulness. This primer will invite you to do both. It will assume you already know something, or at least believe something, about teaching and learning. This assumption may not be as simple as it seems, since you may take a lot of your knowledge about education for granted or describe it in terms other than *teaching* and *learning*. Therefore, in the remainder of this chapter, I try to point to some of what you may already know and believe, the ideas that you can thus contribute to a dialogue on teaching and learning.

What Do You Already Know About Teaching and Learning?

You probably already have significant knowledge about teaching and learning. You may not recognize it as such, though, because some parts consist of *assumptions* you hold about these activities, whereas other parts may be expressed in terms not typical of educational dialogues (Seifert, 1992; Seifert & Handziuk, 1993). To see what I mean, consider a number of topics about which you probably already have views:

- The nature of children and youth
- How people change as they grow older
- The nature of learning and of thinking

Chances are you already have views about these topics, each of which has a lot to do with teaching and learning. What do *you* think children and young people are like? How do they change over time? What do *you* mean when you say they "learn" or "think"? You may even have views about whether these are the most important questions to ask in the first place. When you stop and think, one question may seem more important than another; or you may feel that one topic or question should be phrased differently. Before you read further in this chapter, therefore, you might take a moment to reflect on how you would respond to each question. Or, if possible, talk to a friend or classmate about your views. Your ideas will be your particular starting point in constructing a psychology of teaching and learning. The ideas from classmates, from teachers, and from this primer probably will not be your ending point, but they will assist you in deciding on directions in which to expand your beliefs.

In Your Own Voice

I'm trying to make reasonable assumptions here about areas where you have prior knowledge, but they are still just assumptions.

Is there a better set of headings than these three, one that more closely fits your way of thinking about education?

The Nature of Children and Youth

Underlying any ideas about teaching and learning are assumptions about the nature of children and of young people: beliefs about human nature. One assumption is that children are capable of making decisions for themselves. In some situations, this is obviously true: ask an eight-year-old to choose a flavor for her ice cream cone, and she will almost surely be able to decide. But in other settings, a child's decision-making ability is more suspect. Is a kindergartner capable of deciding whether to attend school each day? Is a ninth-grader capable of deciding whether to engage in sexual intercourse? Between the extremes are decisions of ambiguous status. Can a third-grade student decide whether to spend more time reading a novel or learning science? Teachers, parents, and even students themselves disagree in answering this question. The reasons for the disagreement vary, but they all center on assumptions about a key issue: whether or not children can indeed make decisions for themselves.

Another assumption about the nature of children has to do with their inherent stability: do children have an "essence" that is basically fixed and stable or one that is changeable? Obviously some things about children do change—for example, they grow taller, their skills may shift sometimes even from day to day, and they may seem more competent (hopefully) from year to year. But are these changes merely superficial, or do they signify deeper, more profound alterations? To take an example that concerns teachers, think about this: if a student's reading skill improves dramatically during the course of schooling, does this mean the student is becoming *essentially* more intelligent with each passing year or merely more skilled? Perhaps "intelligence" does not grow simply because verbal skills grow; perhaps it remains constant in spite of changes in academic knowledge—or perhaps not. Teachers (and others who observe children) disagree about these possibilities. The disagreement may appear to be about the nature of intelligence, but it is really about something more: the fundamental stability of human beings. Are you the same yesterday, today, and tomorrow? You probably already have something to say about this matter.

How People Change as They Get Older

The problem of stability versus change suggests a related area in which you probably already have beliefs and assumptions—one that has to do not with *whether* people change as they get older but *how* or by what process. Obviously older individuals can do some things that younger ones cannot; with age, you learn to talk, catch a ball, read a book, and (perhaps) invite a friend to visit. But how do such changes come about? Is each change a response to specific events and relatively unrelated to other changes? Sometimes this must surely be true: it is hard (though perhaps not impossible) to imagine how learning to catch a ball will influence learning to read a book. The two changes seem rather unrelated, at least on the face of it. But what about learning to talk, learning to read, and learning to write? Those activities seem more related; therefore, maybe they have some underlying cause, and developing talent in one might improve talent in the other. But only up to a point. You may have met someone who talks better than he or she writes or who writes better than he or she talks. In fact, maybe you are one of those people yourself.

In any case, you probably make assumptions not only about *what* changes occur with age but also about *how* the changes come about (Overton, 1991). One common assumption, for example, is that change is like the growth of a seed or a plant: it occurs not in discrete bits but in complex, interlocking patterns, as when a seed sprouts or a flower blossoms forth. From this perspective, learning to talk and learning to read might be parts of a larger process of change, one that is part of a general pattern of language development and unfolds in a predictable way. A second common assumption is that human change is like the functioning of a finely tuned machine such as a clock or a computer. Separate changes (such as talking, reading, and writing) may only appear to be related; in reality, they may unfold together because of specific but separate influences. The chime on a grandfather clock, for example, often runs off of a different spring than the minute and hour hands on the clock; the hands may trigger the chime periodically, but in principle each could run without the other. In a similar way, a student may learn to talk, read, and write separately, even though one skill may trigger or make use of the others some of the time.

Even if you have not thought explicitly about how people change, you may already have used ideas such as these when you think or talk about *teaching* and *learning*. When you speak of a student being "ready" for a new learning experience, for example, you may be assuming that change consists of a process of patterned growth. To say that Joe is "ready" to begin kindergarten or that you are "ready" to begin college is to say that a number of changes have occurred simultaneously and somewhat predictably. When you speak of "improving your writing skills," on the other hand, you are more likely to be assuming that discrete, separate skills exist, could have been acquired separately, and can now be finetuned and performed separately as well. It is common, in fact, to speak of human change in one way on some occasions and in another way on others. Such "inconsistency" is not a problem in thinking about teaching and learning, as long as you are aware of its occurrence. The real challenge is to make yourself aware of your own diversity.

The Nature of Learning and of Thinking

When you or I speak of *learning*, we are likely to have a metaphor in mind, a comparison of learning to a familiar object or activity (Bullough, Knowles & Crow, 1992). Sometimes learning is compared to a telephone network: you learn when you "make connections," as if multiple phone calls were criss-crossing your brain. Sometimes learning is compared to a bank: you "add to your storehouse of knowledge," making deposits and withdrawals as needed but otherwise letting your knowledge remain dormant and unused. Or learning may be likened to a job (you learn if there is a payoff, such as course credit or praise from your instructor), to eating (you "digest" ideas), or to combat (you are "challenged" to "master" the curriculum). These and other images serve different purposes in dialogues about learning; they are used with reference to different learning situations, curricula, and students. Maybe you can think of other metaphors or likenesses you have sometimes used. Some are probably shared with your friends and classmates, but others may be unique to you. *Learning*, it seems, does not mean the same thing to everyone.

Likewise, you probably already have views about **thinking**. Stop for a moment and consider this term. You may believe from experience, for example, that thinking is essentially equivalent to language: you often think silently in words or even openly talk to yourself when you are thinking hard. Or you may believe thinking is visual: sometimes you think in pictures, imagining an event, a place, or a person (e.g., "I'm trying to picture myself as a teacher"). Or thinking may seem equivalent to physical action, such as dodging quickly out of the way of a student charging down the hallway; "Quick thinking," you compliment yourself, as if thought were a matter of agility. *Thinking*, like learning, is like a chameleon, changing colors to fit its surroundings.

You may also regard thinking as a process that happens "inside" you. Most of us speak of "my" thoughts and "my" plans; yet it is hard not to notice how much your thoughts and plans are shaped by other individuals or events outside yourself. In the morning, you think about what to buy a friend for a birthday present, and decide to get something that day. But events at work—or, more precisely, the people there—distract you. You forget to go shopping after work. The next day you write yourself a note as a reminder to go shopping. This succeeds in reminding you, except that the store clerk shows you something better than what you had planned on buying—but also more expensive. You hesitate, and end up not getting anything that day. That night you are so tired from the extra shopping that you forget to write yourself another reminder note, and as a result you forget to act on the birthday present "problem," as it has now become, for two more days. Time is now running out, so you settle for something less desirable and less expensive than you had first planned. You end up annoyed with yourself: you seem forgetful and a poor planner! In taking responsibility for forgetting, though, you assume your plans have been "in" you all along rather than also "in" the daily world in which you participated. You therefore experience the distractions and delays as invasions instead of as transactions for which you are only partly responsible. You assume exclusive ownership of your plans, but in reality the plans have changed in focus and importance in response to events and other people as well as in response to you. In a very real sense, then, the thinking that went into your plans "belonged" to everyone, not just to you.

Taking Your Existing Beliefs and Knowledge Seriously

I intend to take your existing beliefs and knowledge about teaching and learning seriously. I will do so in three ways. First, I will continually invite you to reflect on what you know and on the reasons for your beliefs. Second, I will attempt to express my own knowledge and beliefs as explicitly as possible. I will try, of course, to be fair to viewpoints other than my own, but I will also not try to pretend that I have no views of my own or that this primer offers a "God's-eye view" of teaching and learning. Third, I will deliberately present a range of ideas, concepts, and theories about how learning occurs and how knowledge is constructed. These will vary in how much they either support or challenge your existing views about teaching and learning. Simply by showing you the variety, though, I hope to communicate a respect for differences of opinion, including your own. Whatever else you gain from reading this primer, I hope you will discover that psychological and educational research is itself a human creation—a systematic one, perhaps, but one that is not eternally fixed.

What Lies Ahead

*I*N the rest of this primer, I will explore major themes or topics that bear on the ideas of *teaching* and *learning*. But my explorations will make sense only if you participate in them: this journey is one that we must make together. For this reason, I have designed the chapters to invite your thoughtful response. I hope you take up my invitation.

Explorations

The topics of this primer come from issues and problems experienced in classrooms and situations related to classrooms. Chapters 1 and 4 frame the entire primer by exploring what you bring to teaching, how you might decide how to grow and develop as a professional, and where you might get information and support for your decisions. The difference between the two chapters is in the directions in which they look. Chapter 1 invites you to look at yourself now—at your current strengths and sources of support. Chapter 4 looks to your future and/or current teacher situation—at choices you will need and want to make as a professional, and at resources to mobilize for making the choices successfully.

Chapters 2 and 3 both support and test the framework offered in the other two chapters, by discussing two key problems about teaching. Chapter 2 looks at how students think, with special emphasis on the incredible variety of their thinking skills and of the ways that we as teachers might regard those skills. Chapter 3 looks at how we, as teachers, can learn from our experience systematically through forms of research planned and conducted by teachers themselves. The "teacher research" described in Chapter 3 is hard work. As the examples there suggest, though, it is not only feasible, but especially valuable for assisting teachers in finding their own ways as professionals.

Invitations to Respond

As you read about these topics, I invite you to respond in a number of ways. The most obvious is by **asking you questions** as I go along: prompting you to think about your own views on the major problems of teaching and learning. Sometimes I embed one of these questions in the text itself, and other times I highlight it in a special box called "In Your Own Voice." Where I place the question, though, is less important than whether you take up the invitation to respond. Unless you grapple with issues of teaching and learning, you cannot construct a useful framework for your later work as a teacher. Remember: inside my questions are issues, not simple facts. Reasonable people, including yourself and others like you, can expect to disagree about the answers.

Another way I invite you to participate is by **providing commentary from teachers and researchers** about key topics. Their comments are highlighted in boxes called "Multiple Voices." The commentators include both persons widely published and known in the field of education, and persons well known primarily to the students in their own classrooms. Including both confirms that useful knowledge comes from many sources, only one of which is educational research. Useful knowledge also comes from successful teaching and honest reflection on teaching practices. In this important sense, we are all—yourself included—responsible for constructing the psychology of teaching and learning.

Other ways in which I invite your participation operate more indirectly. For example, each chapter opens with a **concept map,** called Chapter View, showing how key ideas or themes from the chapter fit together. But I intentionally leave the concept map sketchy or incomplete at the beginning of the chapter and invite you to fill in its gaps or even rearrange it fundamentally. At the end of each chapter the concept map appears again, but this time it's called Chapter Re-View and shows my version of how it might be made more complete. As you will see, there will often be more than one way to complete a concept map; mine will be only one of them, though hopefully it will be a thoughtful one.

Finally, I extend an indirect invitation through a stylistic feature of this primer, its heavy **use of narrative or "stories"** about teaching. I have deliberately used narrative because I believe narrative is how most of us actually think about teaching and learning (Bruner, 1990; Phillips, 1994). The stories are based on real-life concerns about teaching and learning, but do not describe real people or incidents. To an extent, therefore, the line between fiction and fact will be blurred for these stories, just as it often is in memories of real life.

Like many stories, the ones in this primer often have more than one interpretation. Most of the time, I have tried to indicate the interpretations that I intended. But since other meanings may lurk in the wings, I often invite you to explore alternative interpretations and how they relate to your own views on teaching and learning. Indirectly, then, the stories ultimately invite participation; they ask for a dialogue among you, me, and the characters.

CHAPTER RE-VIEW

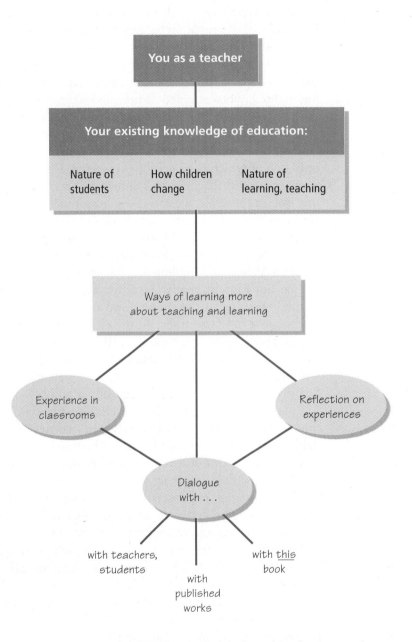

Chapter Re-View: Starting with Your Experience and Knowledge This Chapter Re-View suggests directions in which the chapter might have taken your thinking—though, of course, other directions are also possible. It expands the Chapter View, which suggests a starting point, conceptually, for the chapter. But this Re-View does not suggest an ending point. Like the Chapter View, it represents just one perspective among many.

Key Terms and Concepts

constructivism (4)   learning (3)   teaching (3)
dialogue (10)   reflection (6)   thinking (18)

Annotated Readings

Dewey, John. (1933/1998). *How we think: A restatement of the relation of reflective thinking to the educative process.* Boston: Houghton Mifflin. A classic about the importance of reflection for becoming a highly skilled teacher. The language is sometimes a bit quaint (it was first published 65 years ago), but the ideas are still sound.

Hansen, David. (1995). *The call to teach.* New York: Teachers College Press. Accounts of three teachers who work under difficult conditions (e.g., because they have students who are at high risk for failure) and the sense they make of their work and of their own motives for teaching.

Schön, Donald. (1987). *Educating the reflective practitioner.* San Francisco: Jossey-Bass.

Schön, Donald. (1985). *The reflective practitioner.* New York: Basic Books. Donald Schön offers some of the best explanations of how practitioners think when they work in ever-changing, "messy" professions, including (but not limited to) education. He makes good suggestions for helping practitioners in these areas become more skilled at reflection.

Internet Resources

<www.classroom.net> Newsletters, videos, books, and interactive "chat" lines for discussing issues with teachers of all kinds.

<www.newmaine.com/progressive-educator> Materials about innovative approaches to teaching and learning, as well as an interactive "chat" line.

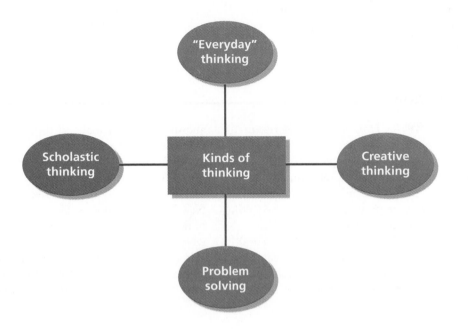

Chapter View: Thinking About Thinking This Chapter View is a concept map that indicates one among many ways of thinking about the chapter. It suggests a starting point, conceptually, for the chapter but is incomplete by itself. At the end of the chapter is a Chapter Re-View, which expands on the Chapter View, suggesting directions for taking your thinking further—though, of course, other directions are also possible.

2
Thinking About Thinking

Most people already have beliefs about what "thinking" consists of, especially when it has to do with classrooms and schools. For one thing, *thinking* is supposed to differ from feelings and emotions. We speak of "cold, hard" reasoning; if we say that someone's thinking is "soft," we are likely to be criticizing. *Thinking* is also supposed to be a general process, distinct from *what* you think about. Just as my computer can organize and process almost any possible string of words, so my mind should be able, in principle, to think about any possible topic or event: to say that an idea is "unthinkable" means only that we have strong negative feelings about it or conventions against public discussion of it, not that we cannot actually contemplate it. In structure, therefore, *thinking* is usually thought of as extremely general, even if in content it sometimes can be very specific. I can think about anything: my pet dog, my childhood, the meaning of my life. In thinking about *thinking,* therefore, we usually envision an activity that is detached from feelings and rather general. These qualities give the concept prestige; we usually believe it is good to be able to *think* well in the sense outlined here.

School-Based and Everyday Thinking Compared

UT how realistic is this commonsense view of thinking, and how helpful is it to teachers? I invite you to consider the possibility that most of the time it is partially misleading, that thinking *is* not usually general or emotionally detached. I invite you to consider, furthermore, that one of the few situations where thinking most often does have these qualities is in school classrooms, in the interactions among teachers, students, and curricula. To an important degree, then, notions of *thinking* are like notions of *learning*, in that they refer to something different inside a classroom than outside. Bridging the gaps between the classroom and the rest of the world therefore becomes part of a teacher's job.

The Math Lesson in Class

Tom and Charleen are doing math in their second-grade class. Their teacher has been following the curriculum, which tells her to put the students in small groups to solve money problems. It also tells her to use small amounts of money; in its words, "children of this age learn best by manipulating tangible materials. They are unable to conceptualize large amounts of money, which are too abstract for them." The teacher has therefore given Tom and Charleen twelve "pennies" in the form of poker chips; their task at this particular moment is to divide the money in various ways to see how many combinations of candy they can buy from a price list the teacher has given them. The children are reasonably content as they work on the task, though they giggle a lot as they record their results.

"Can't buy much for 12 cents, can you?" says Tom to Charleen.

"Nope," she replies, "and anyway my mom and dad never let me buy candy ever, 'cept on my birthday." They continue working a few more minutes, experimenting with various combinations of poker chip "pennies." Then they record their results and wait.

Tom's Math Lesson at Home

Later, after school, Tom is home with his younger brother watching "junk" TV to pass the time before his mom gets home from work. Tom and his brother live with their mother; they barely know their father, who left home when Tom was about three years old. Today they have been watching cartoons, a practice their mom frowns on but tolerates for times when she is not at home. Today's cartoon show has been aggressively advertising a computer game called Space Blasters.

"Can I have Space Blasters for my birthday?" Tom asks his mom. He thinks this is a simple question, but he is wrong.

"Are you kidding?" says his mom. Her eyes widen and her voice becomes slow and measured. "One of those games costs almost $100! Do you have any idea how much money that is?" She stares hard at Tom, waiting for an answer.

"No, ma'am," Tom murmurs, trying suddenly to sound respectful. "I guess it's a lot . . . ?"

"Darn right it is!," says mom. "It's two weeks of groceries—that's what it is. Or all of your clothes to start school. Or our trip to see grandpa this Christmas!"

Tom withdraws to the living room again and shuts off the TV. "Mom's in one of her moods," he tells his younger brother. Privately, he can't decide whether he has actually done something wrong. Clearly amounts of money *do* matter and have consequences. Clearly, too, $100 is "a lot"—equivalent in consequences to several major activities he is familiar with.

Charleen's Math Lesson at Home

After school, Charleen is grocery shopping with her teenage sister. Charleen lives with her sister and both parents, but her parents work most evenings as caretakers for a building downtown. This particular evening, the two girls must buy food for the family for the coming week, and Charlene's special task is to choose breakfast cereal. She knows without being told that she should find the "best buy," meaning the most cereal at the lowest cost; her family is not poor, but she has been told, directly and indirectly, that money does need to be conserved carefully.

Charleen studies the cereal aisle closely. She has discovered that prices are posted on a small sticker under each type of cereal: an overall price in moderate-size print and a price per ounce in tiny print. The family's favorite type of cereal (bran flakes) happens to be on sale ($2) on one brand but not on another ($3). She starts to take the cheaper brand, but then peers closely at the prices and boxes. She notices that the box on sale is *smaller* than the other box. She hesitates.

Maybe the larger box is really a better buy? she wonders. She notes the quantity in each box: the on-sale box is 12 ounces, and the regular box is 14. That doesn't seem like much of a difference, she thinks.

In the end she takes two of the smaller boxes, though together they will cost more than a single box of the larger size. She takes them to her sister, feeling a bit nervous about her choice.

Charleen is relieved to find that her sister is happy with her choice. "You did right," says her sister. "These will be cheaper in the long run, and we'll get through both boxes eventually." Then she mutters, "Stupid grocery store. You almost have to have a calculator to figure out the *real* prices!"

Charleen feels a brief moment of pride at having succeeded in selecting this particular "best buy," but she's not sure whether she'll be able to do it again the next time she must choose from among prices, quantities, and sizes. Clearly, though, Charleen realizes that discerning prices is a serious business, that it must take skill if even her big sister has trouble doing it, and that she had better learn how to do it even if it *is* hard.

In Your Own Voice

As a student, presumably you've had extensive experience in thinking!

Some has been done in class (hopefully), but a lot has been done outside.

For you, how has thinking in class differed from thinking outside?

Do the differences coincide with my comments here or not?

As these examples suggest, there are differences between thinking as it occurs in classrooms and thinking as it occurs elsewhere. In classrooms, what counts officially as thinking is likely to be tied to specific problems set by a curriculum. Furthermore, the problems are likely to be sequenced in ways specified by the curriculum or by a teacher, either of which has usually based the sequencing on beliefs, metaphors, and theories of how children learn best. In learning about money, for example, Tom and Charleen were asked to deal with very small amounts, presumably on the grounds that small amounts would be easier for them to comprehend. Ironically, though, this curricular strategy may have made the money activity seem less important and motivating; as Tom said, "Can't buy much for 12 cents, can you?"

Outside classrooms, thinking often takes on a different character: there it is likely to be an emotional event as well as an intellectual one. Discussing the cost of Space Blasters, for example, involves serious financial issues for Tom's mother and therefore for Tom. So does Charleen's search for the best buy in breakfast cereals. Both children experience significant worries about money at the same time they learn important lessons about what money is for, how much it can buy, and consequences of various uses of money. These lessons are determined not by a curriculum or by theoretical images of learning but by the children's family circumstances. More well-to-do families might not show as much concern about costs, and different lessons in thinking might therefore be taught, at least lessons about money.

These contrasts do not mean that school-based thinking is always too tame and isolated from life; rather, it means that teachers inevitably face a problem of **transfer** of learning, or getting students to apply knowledge acquired in one situation to another, related situation. It is not good enough to be able to count money in class, as Tom and Charleen did; you should be able to count it at the store as well. It is not good enough to be able to read books and materials provided by your teacher; you should be able to read books and materials that you freely choose from the library or elsewhere. And so on. The challenge of transfer can be large, small, or anywhere in between. It may be relatively easy to induce students to use arithmetic skills learned in class to solve highly similar arithmetic problems on a unit test—unless a student lacks motivation to pass the test. It can be hard to motivate them to use their knowledge of high school chemistry in any situation other than the chemistry class itself—unless, of course, a student is planning a career as a chemist. Hard or easy, though, the problem of inducing transfer remains. Therefore, we return to it from various directions in later chapters. Sometimes it will reappear as a problem of motivating students, or of the similarity between life in the classroom and life in the community, or of observing the results of learning appropriately. In the meantime, it is important to clarify what you, I, or any other teacher means when we say we "understand students' thinking" and note how that phrase can mean different things in different situations.

A Thumbnail Sketch of Thinking

*L*ET's look at three kinds of thinking in turn, then compare them with one another. First, we'll examine thinking that is generally considered "the" kind needed for school: thinking as scholastic aptitude. In our particular society, this form of thinking is often associated not only with high grades but also with high performance on standardized tests of scholastic aptitude and intelligence. Because of this historic association, we will also discuss the nature and purposes of such tests and how they have affected beliefs about what "good thinking" is, both in classrooms and out.

After considering the kind of thinking needed for success on tests of scholastic aptitude, we will consider two alternative forms: problem solving and creativity. *Problem solving* refers to the ways students (and teachers) deal with complex, ill-defined situations requiring solutions. *Creativity* refers to the ways people come up with innovative but still useful ideas and products. Together scholastic aptitude, problem solving, and creativity represent three major, distinct elements of what most of us think of as *thinking*. They also pose distinct challenges and opportunities for teachers, partly because of the conditions of teaching and of classroom life, which make some kinds of activities, conversations, and goals easier to arrange than others.

In Your Own Voice

As you think about *thinking* in reading this chapter, you might consider how much *you* value scholastic aptitude, problem solving, and creativity in your own life.

Don't limit yourself to your classroom life when you do this; think about *all* of your experiences: home, family, friends, job—everything.

Paper-and-pencil tests are so widespread, and have such a long history, that it is tempting to equate performance on them with what students actually learn.
© Michael Newman/Photo Edit

Thinking as Scholastic Aptitude

ONE way to think of thinking is as scholastic aptitude: the skills needed to succeed in school, earn high grades, and the like. What might these skills be? One clue to this question comes from the many standardized tests designed to predict school success (Berlak, 1993; Frederikson, Mislevy & Bejar, 1993). Because of their purpose, they tend to call for the kind of thinking expected in school: verbal and numerical reasoning, as well as general "worldly knowledge" as shown, in particular, by having a large vocabulary. The following questions are typical in requiring these forms of thinking; they are similar to items (or questions) in the Stanford-Binet Test of Intelligence (Thorndike, Hagen & Sattler, 1986), one of the most widely used and respected tests for predicting scholastic aptitude:

- For a grade-school child: "Why is this foolish? 'A man had the flu twice. The first time it killed him, but the second time he got well quickly.'"
- For a high-school youth: "How are these alike: winter and summer; happy and sad; much and little?"

- For an adult: "Let's suppose that this box has two smaller boxes inside it, and each one of the smaller boxes contains a little tiny box. How many boxes are there altogether, counting the big one?"
- For an adult: "What does this proverb mean? 'Let sleeping dogs lie.'"

Do these questions seem vaguely familiar, as if you have seen something like them somewhere before? If so, the reason may be that you have been asked questions of this general "style" or type during your career as a student (though probably not these exact questions). The underlying style is widespread in public schooling and is characterized by the following qualities:

- The test item asks you to solve a problem or answer a question someone else has created rather than one you have set for yourself.
- It poses a problem that tends to have a specific answer or "correct" solution rather than one that has a number of alternative solutions.
- It requires you to read carefully (or sometimes listen carefully) to the exact wording of the problem or question.
- It rewards you for having knowledge of many terms and words, including several that are rarely used in everyday conversation.
- It expects you to solve the problem or answer the question by yourself, without consultation with peers or experts.

Altogether, the underlying qualities imply an image of *thinking*, one that depicts thinking as part of school learning and school success. As you might suspect, this view is not the only view of *thinking*; in fact, most thinking done outside of school does not have these qualities (Resnick, 1987; Resnick, Levine & Teasley, 1991). Nonetheless, the idea of *thinking* as scholastic aptitude is widely believed and respected in our society. How complete, useful, and fair this idea is will ultimately be up to you to decide; it will not necessarily be good for you simply because others believe it already. Because you should make up your mind intelligently, though, and because a school-based view of *thinking* is indeed so prominent, you should first consider it as accurately and fairly as possible. A good way to do so is to look a bit more closely at one of its sources of supports: standardized tests of scholastic aptitude.

Tests of Scholastic Aptitude

Most standardized tests of aptitude include school-like questions such as those already mentioned, questions about verbal reasoning, numerical skills, and vocabulary. It is not the content or style of the questions, however, that qualifies them as indicators of thinking as scholastic aptitude; it is the fact that they identify students who perform well in school. Since this amounts to defining scholastic aptitude strictly by its function, a long-lasting debate (now spanning more than a century) has developed about how to define it in terms of its content or "essence" (Horn, 1989).

A Single, Global Ability?

One school of thought proposes interpreting scholastic aptitude as a single, general quality or trait within individuals, one often called "general intelligence" and abbreviated for convenience with the single letter g. In this view, g (alias scholastic aptitude) is a quantity of which each of us has some amount. The amount is either inherited genetically, acquired and fixed early in life, or a mixture of both (Herrnstein & Murray, 1994). Put in crass terms, some people are smarter than others and always will be; school performance and scholastic aptitude tests merely reflect that fact. Teachers' job, therefore, is to adjust their expectations to fit the inevitable differences among students so that everyone can learn "to the best of his or her ability." Although most teachers feel this sentiment at one time or another, note something important about it: what's being talked about here is a *single, global* ability that governs performance in many areas, not a single, particular ability that influences only specific areas of performance.

One Talent Among Many?

A competing view of scholastic aptitude is that it is one among several important thinking abilities or "intelligences," each contributing to different forms of success in life. Scholastic aptitude is important because it contributes to school or academic success in particular, but as a term it is both too general and too specific. It may be too general because several more specific kinds of talent may create success in school; remembering facts, for example, may require a different kind of thinking than knowing how to plan your study time (Sternberg, 1990). It may be too specific, though, because some forms of thinking may be unrelated to scholastic aptitude and therefore rarely get honored fully in school: creative musical or artistic talents, for example, or sensitivity to the needs of others (Gardner, 1993). A successful student may have these attri-

In Your Own Voice

Gradually I've discovered that lots of people have talents that are not recognized in school.

Mine was the piano: I was pretty good at it, but there was no way for me to translate that talent into school grades or to gain more than passing recognition at occasional school talent shows.

What about you?

What can you do, and what qualities do you have, that go unnoticed, or undernoticed, at school?

butes, but not necessarily. Teachers and classmates may appreciate these qualities in a student when they see them, but these abilities rarely get as much credit as talents in the more traditional curricular areas, such as language arts or mathematics.

The Experience of Being Tested

The latter interpretation—viewing thinking as a mixture of scholastic aptitudes—seems the more useful for understanding the full diversity of talents among students, but unfortunately it is full of ambiguity. The problem is that students' behaviors and achievements usually represent several skills or talents at once, and how are you to identify which ones they are displaying on any one occasion? On a particular test of scholastic aptitude, for example, a student may make dozens of responses; but do these show reading ability, reasoning ability, a cooperative attitude toward taking tests, or something else? Interpreting test responses can be a bit like watching a night sky full of stars: you can always "see" several patterns among the same overall set of stars, each of which may be right or convenient for certain purposes. Consider these four high school students as they encounter a particular item on a multiple-choice test of scholastic aptitude:

Question #25: Water lilies double in area every 24 hours. At the beginning of the summer, there is one water lily on a lake. The lake covers exactly 10,000 square feet. It takes 60 days for the lake to become covered with water lilies completely. On what day is the lake half covered?
- *a) day 20*
- *b) day 30*
- *c) day 45*
- *d) day 59*

Yolanda has taken advanced math courses in high school, and she recognizes the problem as one of exponential growth: it's something to do with logarithms and exponents, she says to herself. She sets about trying to determine the logarithmic formula for this problem, hoping she can calculate how many days from the beginning are needed to cover the lake halfway.

But finding this formula proves very difficult. Eventually Yolanda simply guesses at a formula, calculates an answer of "53 days," and picks option d (day 59) because it is the closest numerically and because she expects that the answer should not be a number divisible by 5. Yolanda has the distinct impression both that her guess is wrong and that she has spent too much time on the problem.

In Your Own Voice

I notice that Yolanda, Paul, and Morris are spending a lot of time—perhaps too much—on this problem.

My instinct is to coach them on the test-taking strategy of "not taking too much time on any one problem."

But might this just encourage them to move too quickly through problems and to think superficially?

Paul has never seen a water lily in his life, so he spends valuable time trying to imagine what one looks like. He has the idea that if he can understand something about lilies, it might help him to solve the problem. Maybe, he thinks, the question is not really as mathematical as it appears; maybe lilies grow in a special way or at some special fixed rate, and if I could just figure these out, I could solve the problem quickly. Eventually he gives up and picks option b (day 30) because it is halfway between day 0 and day 60.

Morris is skeptical about tests. Surely, he says to himself, this question is a trick. He believes test makers would not really ask about exponents on a test of general ability, since not enough students know about them. What, then, is the trick? He agonizes over this question for a long time without success. Finally, at the last minute, he has an idea. If the lake is full on day 60, the terms of the problem imply that it must have been exactly half full on the day before, that is, on day 59. He considers option d (day 59), but decides against it because the last three questions on the test have been option d. So he picks option c at random and moves on.

Angela has always liked "clever" thought problems and feels familiar with this one even though she has never seen it before. It's like those "backwards reasoning" ones I saw in the library book last month, she thinks. Start at the end and work back: day 60 is full of lilies, so day 59 must be half full. She chooses option d (day 59) and moves on to the next problem.

These four students show some of the ambiguities of equating *thinking* with scholastic aptitude. Because this view is ultimately based on standardized testing, it contains the ambiguities of test-taking behaviors (Kamii, 1990; Perrone, 1991). Among the four students, Yolanda and Angela respond correctly, but for very different reasons; Paul and Morris respond incorrectly, but also for different reasons. Whether correct or not, responses on a standardized test are ambiguous, that is, have more than one possible meaning. Errors can occur because of

1. Thinking about or framing the problem inappropriately (as Yolanda did)
2. Lack of experience with a particular problem or type of problem (Paul)
3. Lack of motivation and daydreaming
4. Unlucky guessing (e.g., Morris, who has been conditioned to expect tricks)
5. Combinations of these and other influences

Successes can result from

1. Familiarity or experience with a problem (Angela)

2. Lucky guessing (Yolanda)

3. Erroneous methods of solution that nonetheless lead to a correct answer

4. A combination of these and other influences

Note, though, that these ambiguities do not invalidate the test of scholastic aptitude for its original purpose. If the test is intended to predict overall success in school in particular, and if it has been well constructed, the overall test results will indeed predict school success: high-scoring people will be more likely to do well in school, at least as schools traditionally have been organized and taught. This point applies to Yolanda, Paul, Morris, and Angela as much as to other individuals. Give them one hundred more problems that resemble school thinking tasks, such as the water lily problem, and their performances will suggest which of them is most successful academically. "What" they actually think in solving the one hundred problems, though, will still be uncertain.

To understand the nature of *thinking*, then, we will have to look in places other than standardized tests of scholastic aptitude, in spite of their historical importance in education. What if we looked at classroom events themselves? Would they show more than tests about what thinking "really" is? What if we saw activities in classrooms, for example, that required students to construct knowledge for themselves on their own initiative or to piece it together in collaboration with classmates and others?

Joe paused after reading the paragraph above, thinking about *thinking* in a classroom. Across town his friend Sara did the same: she took a break to think about *thinking*. Here is what each of them imagined:

Joe: A third-grade class—my third-grade class: Mrs. Kennedy, my favorite teacher of all time! We are doing two-digit subtraction problems: 43 − 26 = . . . ? She lets us write down the problem and work on it before answering. We all scribble numbers madly. Then I've got it! I raise my hand and announce my answer: 23. "No, Joe,

Sara: Senior high; tenth-grade English. Mr. Vittetoe has told us to write a short story—"not more than 5 pages long," he said. I am writing just now; getting a sore wrist, in fact. But also it's not going anywhere, and I have just realized that. It had started out as an account of a girl running away to Canada. But it's stupid; no one

In Your Own Voice

When I reread this section, it seemed as though I was implying that skill at standardized tests is undesirable.

Indeed, I think that is true in some ways but not others.

To think about how "test-wiseness" can be good, read the novel *Stand and Deliver* by Nicholas Edwards (1989), or see the film by the same name.

The story describes the work of Jaime Escalante, a teacher in an inner-city neighborhood with students who were at risk for failure.

He coached the students to outstanding success on college entrance aptitude tests and in so doing made a remarkable difference in their lives.

think again," says Mrs. Kennedy courteously. I look at my scribbles: I had reversed the digits in the "ones" column. She was asking us to "borrow," something we had just learned. I do more scribbles; "17," I say, without being called on.

ever "runs away to Canada." I sit there frustrated, not knowing whether to tear up my draft or shed a tear. What to do? Just then Mr. Vittetoe walks by; sees me. "Let's talk about it," he says. "Tell me your idea for the story." So we begin talking.

In homes on opposite sides of town, Joe and Sara daydream a moment longer about their separate examples. Separately, they both remark to themselves: funny how there's frustration in it, but also satisfaction, and social interaction. I wonder if my example is OK. And then they think: it's good that no one will see *my* example. It's probably not typical.

In response to my invitation to "imagine a time in class that showed a good example of thinking," Joe and Sara have both pictured examples of *problem solving,* a way of thinking about *thinking* quite different from the perspective based on testing scholastic aptitude. Even though both belittle their examples, they may be sensing something important— noticing another kind of thinking that deserves a closer look.

Thinking as Problem Solving

*S*UPPOSE that instead of defining *thinking* by what schooling requires, we defined it more broadly, by the requirements of various human occupations and everyday activities. What would *thinking* look like then? Considerable research has been done from this broader perspective, with *thinking* more often being called **problem solving,** the analysis and solution of situations that pose difficulties, inconsistencies, or obstacles of some kind. The research on problem solving both complicates and clarifies the scholastically based notion of thinking: some types of problem solving rarely occur in classrooms, either because they are impractical to arrange in classrooms or because they are not traditionally part of the school curriculum. On the other hand, as the examples devised by Joe and Sara show, much problem solving *does* occur in classrooms and may indeed be recognized as such by teachers. Looking at nonschool settings helps to put classroom think-

In classroom problem solving, as in this science experiment, students are likely to know what they are looking for and how to go about looking for it. Neither condition is as certain for problem solving outside of classroom settings.
© Gale Zucker/Stock Boston

In Your Own Voice

Before reading further, take a minute to imagine a time that, for you, showed "good" thinking.

Remember everything about it: who was thinking, what was being thought about, the circumstances of the incident, who else was present, and what made the thinking happen.

Keep this memory in mind as you read on; ask yourself later whether you still consider your image an example of "good" thinking.

ing in perspective and to avoid the temptation to equate classroom activities with thinking itself—to believe that thinking is equivalent to completing worksheets or answering recitation-style questions. Looking at out-of-school examples also suggests qualities of problem solving that teachers need to import into classroom activities so that "good" thinking occurs there as well.

Kinds of Problem Solving

Since problem solving is embedded in everyday activities, it varies a lot from one situation to another. Knowing some of the variations makes it easier to understand how you might encourage problem solving in a classroom, even when the circumstances are quite different than outside of school (Hunt, 1991; Sternberg & Frensch, 1991). Look briefly at the following examples, which describe how a doctor, manager, lawyer, and psychologist solve problems. Then let's figure out what each of these problem solvers has in common with students' problem solving in classrooms.

Diagnosing X-rays

Imagine how a doctor might examine the chest X-rays of a patient. The patient may have a collapsed lung or lung cancer—or perhaps nothing wrong at all. The doctor cannot be sure, and the X-ray pictures give only fuzzy, ambiguous results. The problem is to decide whether the patient really does have something wrong with her lungs and what her medical problem may be.

What makes for good *problem solving* in this situation? Research studies have addressed this question by observing expert radiologists as they talk about X-rays while they diagnose them and comparing their comments with the ones made by inexperienced doctors (Groen & Patel, 1988; Lesgold et al., 1988). In essence the doctors "think out loud" while they work. When this happens, the experts show several important, interrelated differences from the novices:

- Expert radiologists comment on everything in the X-ray of the patient, not just on his or her lungs: *"This looks like a normal female chest, but what's that funny blob there?"*

- Experts begin suggesting general diagnoses more quickly than the novices, but also begin suggesting ways to test their suggestions: *"Left side looks like smoker's lung, or maybe a rib fracture in childhood. Can we ask her about that or at least get another picture from that side?"*

- Experts are more willing to drop initial diagnoses in the face of new, unexpected evidence: *"Oh I didn't know that she had been a star athlete until recently; no wonder her heart looks so big, like it's crowding the lungs."*

- Experts distinguish between relevant and irrelevant information more clearly: *"I might think her lungs were congested, but I can also tell that this picture is badly underexposed; that's probably what makes it so murky."*

These abilities do not necessarily improve steadily with experience. Other observations of medical diagnoses have suggested that certain kinds of cases, especially classic, "textbook" cases, are actually solved better by doctors who are either utterly inexperienced or highly experienced compared to those with moderate experience (Lesgold, 1988). Moderately experienced doctors perform worse with textbook cases, apparently because they are searching for unnecessary complications in these patients. Only the highly experienced doctors (more than ten years of practice) di-

In Your Own Voice

Reading X-rays, of course, is only one kind of problem among many.

How do you think a challenge facing a radiologist differs from the one facing a teacher who must size up a student's learning needs?

agnose well in *all* situations—not only when a patient has an "obvious" problem but also when she or he presents an ambiguous one.

Solving Managerial Problems

A manager of a business faces rather different problems than a medical radiologist. He or she often must deal with many people simultaneously instead of with just one patient at a time, and deal more explicitly with human motives and preferences. Suppose you manage a large grocery store and your selection of coffee has not been selling well; you face the problem of improving the profits on your sales of coffee. How should you do this? You could lower prices (put on a "sale"), but that could also reduce your income; you could invest in more advertising, but that would also cost income; you could put a suggestion box by the coffee display asking customers for suggestions, but the people responding may not be representative of all customers. There is no time for market research on this problem, because each passing day means more money lost on the current selection of coffees. As manager, what should you do?

Studies of problem solving by experienced, skilled managers find they do not take time to analyze this sort of problem consciously and rationally. Instead they tend to act promptly, taking time to reflect only when the consequences of their initial actions begin to unfold (Wagner, 1991). Thinking about the business problem is closely interwoven with acting on the problem. Much of the expertise of management—perhaps even most—seems to consist of acting and responding to business circumstances in appropriate and timely ways; it is skill with procedures rather than skill in terms of conscious, verbal knowledge. You have procedural skills too: when you walk, you simply step forward "in an appropriate and timely way" rather than deliberating on which foot to lift or how far to place it! Only as the consequences of taking the step begin to occur do you reflect on the action: Is the step taking me where I want to go? Did I step in a hidden crack accidentally? These reflections lead to further actions—further steps, in this case.

Finding and Predicting Causes: Lawyers and Psychologists

Lawyers and psychologists show still other patterns of problem solving that differ from those of both managers and doctors, yet are similar in underlying purpose. Both lawyers and psychologists seek the *causes* of human behaviors—the links between earlier actions and later ones—but their orientations differ fundamentally. For lawyers, the major problem is to identify the causes of one specific event and to do so *after* it occurs.

Suppose Jack drives his car into a tree and we now (obviously) know that this mishap has already occurred. As a lawyer, you seek the causes by looking back in time: did the collision happen *because* (1) Jack drank one glass of wine at dinner, or (2) the car manufacturer had installed defective brakes in his car, or (3) Jack's wife was giving birth and Jack needed to get to the hospital? Legal reasoning sorts out these possibilities and presents one chain of causes as more plausible than another (Amsel, Langer & Loutzenhiser, 1991).

For psychologists, in contrast, the major problem is not to account for specific past behaviors but to predict future ones, and to do so in general rather than for specific cases. Think about Jack's collision again. Psychologists would be less concerned than lawyers with why one particular person, Jack, had a traffic accident on one particular occasion. Instead they would focus on general causes and effects: Why do people, including but not limited to Jack, sometimes have traffic accidents? How much are accidents caused *in general* by drinking alcohol, or manufacturing defects, or family crises? Psychologists answer these questions in terms of probabilities: by how likely or unlikely an association is between an earlier event and a later one. Because the associations are phrased in general terms, they allow predictions of future events—or, more precisely, they allow for good guesses and bets about the future.

Commonalities in Problem Solving

The problems solved by doctors, managers, lawyers, and psychologists are diverse, but they have common features, features that suggest ways in which problem solving can and should occur in classrooms (Nye et al., 1988).

For one thing, all four examples require decisions or solutions based on information that is *incomplete* or *ambiguous*. X-rays are fuzzy, consumer purchases have many motivations, criminal actions usually have several possible "causes," and statistical trends never have clear-cut effects on any one person. Yet if one of these problems is to be solved, decisions and understandings must be found anyway.

For another thing, problem solving often takes **educated guesswork**— a form of trial-and-error behavior, but one based on experience and knowledge of the problem rather than on truly random responses. The manager tries a new pricing structure on the basis of thoughtful hunches, but does not know for sure whether the hunches were correct until after he sees the results of his new pricing structure. The doctor guesses at the medical history of the patient, and the psychologist's general predictions about traffic accidents translate into reasonable guesses when applied to individual drivers. Making reasonable guesses takes experience and familiarity with a field: a lawyer tends to solve legal problems more skillfully than a manager. But it also takes deliberate *reflection*, deliberate effort to consider alternatives and assumptions about the nature of a problem and its solutions.

The differences and similarities among problems to be solved raise issues for teachers about *how* to teach problem solving directly (Perkins, 1992). There are enough similarities to tempt us to try teaching problem-solving skills in general: to encourage students to practice "educated guesswork" with certain tasks or assignments, or to practice deciding when they have enough information about a problem to proceed even though the information is not complete. The trouble with this approach, though, is that using it effectively also requires knowledge and information that is very specific and detailed. Estimating the answer to an arithmetic problem, for example, calls for knowledge of certain specific arithmetic facts, not just for knowledge of guesswork strategies. So teachers end up having to foster general problem solving and specific knowledge acquisition simultaneously—which is why teaching can be so challenging!

Problem Solving in the Classroom

In spite of this dilemma about teaching problem solving directly, it is important to realize that genuine problem solving often does occur in classrooms, and at these moments the teacher does have an important contribution to make. Consider what happened in Jerry's classroom:

Jerry listened while his teacher gave the instructions: "Can you connect all of the dots below using only *four* straight lines?" She drew the following display in the middle of the chalkboard:

```
*   *   *

*   *   *

*   *   *
```

Jerry and his classmates stared at the display. Two kids volunteered to try solving it, but they were unsuccessful when they actually tried drawing lines on the board. Jerry stared awhile longer, puzzling over the problem.

When no one seemed to be getting anywhere, the teacher asked, "Think about how you've set the problem up in your mind: think about your *thinking*. Have you made any assumptions about how *long* the lines ought to be?" So Jerry thought—thought about his thinking. He thought especially about how long the lines "ought" to be.

"They need to be no longer than the distance across the square," Jerry said to himself. So he tried several solutions, reproducing the matrix on a piece of paper at his desk. His teacher had encouraged everyone to try as many solutions as possible.

But still he could find no solution, no way to draw only four lines that included all nine dots. He puzzled; he drew; he failed again at it. His teacher saw all of this happening; "Think about what you assume," she said again, "about how long the lines should be."

The teacher encourages actual efforts to solve the problem, even though initial attempts are unsuccessful and have not been fully thought through. She is calling for educated guesswork, for students to draw on their knowledge of other problems of this type.

The teacher encourages reflection on the problem. It is not satisfactory to apply solution methods automatically, without thought.

Now Jerry is trying more solutions, as encouraged by the teacher and as his classmates did earlier. More educated guesswork here. Possibly also a "zone of proximal development," arranged by the teacher, for working on this problem.

So Jerry thought again, and . . . "Aha! She did not actually *say* that the lines could be no longer than the matrix! Why not make them longer?" So he experimented with lines that went beyond the edges, and in just a moment discovered the following solution:

More encouragement to reflect, even to the point of questioning initial solutions.

Soon others in the class had found a solution, although not everyone solved the problem just as Jerry did. "Think about what's happened here," said Jerry's teacher. "Does this problem remind you of any other situations?"

Note that even this relatively simple problem has multiple solutions. It is ambiguous to some extent.

"The dots look like stars," said one of Jerry's classmates. "The lines are the constellations. It's as if there is more than one way to "draw" the constellations in the sky. They don't necessarily have to be drawn the way my science textbook shows them." The teacher nodded.

The teacher encourages students to relate the problem to other situations of interest or concern: helping them to transfer their knowledge back and forth between this problem and others they consider relevant. The notion of transfer is important; see my comments that follow.

"You know what it makes me think of?" said Jerry. "Last year I never felt like I had time for homework because of baseball practice every evening after dinner. I finally figured out that I could still get both things done if I just did some of the homework *before* dinner. I wish I'd thought of it sooner."

The teacher nodded again. "Interesting," she said, "but what's the connection to these dots?"

"Well, it's like I made assumptions about when I had to do homework. I assumed that it all had to fit *after* practice, all in the evening. But I could never make it fit afterward. I finally realized that I had set up the 'problem' wrong: no one had ever actually required me to work only in the evening. My assumption was wrong." The teacher nodded, then smiled.

As in this example, the teacher makes important contributions by asking well-placed questions and in that way guides students toward successful thinking. But the guidance can take a number of forms. The example here implies that the whole class was discussing the problem together. But as Rodelyn Stoeber, a high school science teacher, suggests in the accompanying "Multiple Voices," the teacher can also organize stu-

MULTIPLE VOICES

MULTIPLE VOICES

MULTIPLE VOICES

MULTIPLE VOICES

As a math and science teacher, problem solving is very much a part of my curriculum. From my experience, it is indeed a skill that is difficult to teach. As is mentioned in the chapter, imagination, reflection, and educated guesswork need to be encouraged and developed in students in order for them to become competent in problem solving.

I found Jerry's situation as described in this chapter to be interesting. As a teacher, I think that I would have treated it somewhat differently. I would have had the students address the problem in partners or small groups first, thereby allowing them to discuss and try out their ideas with others. Using this strategy helps students better conceptualize the problem. As there might be several responses to the problem, a sharing of the different solutions as a class would also be a good option. After doing this, students could try to make up their own problems in partners and/or in small groups. However, the teacher needs to gauge students' background knowledge and also create an atmosphere of learning where the students are willing to take risks in sharing their own ideas.

Rodelyn Stoeber, High School Science Teacher, Winnipeg, Canada

dents into small groups prior to a whole-class discussion to stimulate larger amounts of discussion or develop more solutions than a single, large group can accomplish alone.

Who Defines "the" Problem?

There are also differences between this classroom example and the ones described earlier that occurred outside the classroom. Note who defines the problem: to a greater extent than with the professionals described earlier, the students work on a task set not by themselves but by someone else, the teacher. "The" problem therefore means something different for students than for the professionals. To the students, it means finding answers or solutions to a problem to which someone else presumably knows the answer already and then showing this person their success (Denis, Griffin & Cole, 1990). To the professionals, the problem means the same thing, but more: it also means finding and defining the problem in the first place. For a lawyer, for example, "the" problem is not only to explain why a particular traffic accident occurred but also to decide whether it is actually important to create such an explanation.

Transfer

The difference in who finds and defines problems contributes to a problem peculiar to educators, namely how to ensure that students' solutions to tasks in class actually get used on tasks outside class. Educators sometimes call this the problem of *transfer* (Norris, 1992). One obvious way to encourage transfer is to make learning situations as similar as possible to situations where new knowledge or skills will be used. In learning to drive a car, for example, experience behind the wheel may be more helpful than an in-class discussion about driving. The trouble with this strategy, though, is that some forms of performance are difficult to simulate. Teachers can set up a "mock government" to demonstrate how laws are enacted, but making the arrangements takes considerable effort, takes time from other curriculum goals, and may lack some of the drama, tension, and genuine conflict of real government leadership.

Another strategy to encourage transfer was illustrated in the story about Jerry when the teacher makes an explicit effort to get students to relate the classroom task to other situations and problems important to them. As useful as this strategy presumably is, though, it still does not guarantee full use of learning to situations beyond the classroom—full transfer. Students, after all, could merely be learning to *talk* about how a classroom task relates to nonschool tasks. This is a valuable skill, but not the same as learning to make these connections without prompting.

In Your Own Voice

An interesting case in point was Tom and Charleen, the children counting pennies early in this chapter (see p. 26).

Suppose *you* were teaching them.

How could you get them to use their knowledge of counting money outside of class?

And how could you make sure they were not just learning to *talk* about using money outside of class?

Clarity of Problems and Solutions

Another difference between classroom problem solving and much problem solving by professionals has to do with clarity. Outside the classroom, problems more often seem "ill defined": often it is not clear what the problem actually consists of or what a satisfactory solution may be (King & Kitchener, 1994). The store manager may not be selling enough coffee, but he also may not be convinced that coffee is the problem per se; perhaps other features of the store are annoying customers and discouraging purchases, or perhaps the store is not in a commercially strategic part of town, causing fewer people to shop in it. The manager may therefore puzzle over what "the" problem really is before he can know which particular business actions might lead to "solutions." Clarifying the problem requires imagination, not simply the logical application of business principles.

In the classroom problem of the nine dots, on the other hand, the goal is very clear: students are to locate a certain number of lines in a particular way. The orientation of the lines is a bit ambiguous—that is, in fact, "the" problem—but the range of imagination needed to create a solution is relatively restricted. Therefore, if students are to learn problem-solving skills as they are practiced outside of school, they will need tasks that are *more* ambiguous and complex than the nine-dots problem. I suggest some examples of such tasks in the next section.

Thinking as Creativity

*T*HESE comments hint at yet another way you can think about thinking, which is to focus on **creativity,** the making of ideas or things that are genuinely new but also useful or pleasing. Creativity requires a mixture of imagination, logical reasoning, and persistence (Feldman, 1988; Gardner, 1994; Tucke-Bressler, 1992). In the examples of problem solving described in the previous section, all of these qualities may have been present, but our discussion of them emphasized rational or logical activity. With the doctors and their X-rays, for example, we saw how expert doctors engaged in imaginative thinking, which I called "educated guesswork." My emphasis, though, was on the doctors' reasoning skills, on their ability to justify a diagnosis logically. The example of the nine-dot problem showed an even stronger bias

Creativity is not just a matter of doing something unusual. It also involves using familiar materials and solving well-known problems in novel ways, as this girl has done in representing a house with straws.
© Myrleen Ferguson/PhotoEdit

toward logical thinking: students were not so much coming up with a new idea as showing they could find a pre-existing one held by the teacher.

The bias toward thinking as purely logical reasoning is misleading; many human activities *do* create truly new ideas and products, even if they are small ones (Wallace & Gruber, 1992). Consider another classroom activity, one from a fifth-grade class. This one is rather different from the nine-dot task:

Jerry, Brendon, and Kalli looked at the job at hand: they were supposed to make a drawing that "uses five words at random from the dictionary." The instruction sheet told them to write down the first five words they encountered in the dictionary, each from a different page, along with the words' principal definitions. Then they were to let their minds range widely and flexibly to make up connections among the words, even outlandish, improbable connections. The instructions ended cryptically: "Draw something that shows the connections. But take your time; we won't share the drawings until two weeks from now."

For now, though, that last instruction was what the three students were staring at. Frowns and furrowed brows all around; occasional mumbles.

". . . must mean an object? Not a diagram?"

"Can't be done. . . ."

"Must be proving something. But what?"

Hmmm; all three nodded.

Dutifully the three students found five words at random: *dock, keystroke, partridge, ribbon, south.* Other groups did the same and, of course, came up with other lists. Jerry, Brendon, and Kalli brainstormed connections, and behold: they started enjoying it! After their first discussion, they even had a preliminary "picture" in mind: of a partridge with a ribbon around its neck, sitting on a boat dock facing south, typing on a computer.

But Jerry frowned at this first sketch. "It's dorky, too artificial," he said. And the others had to agree. It was a start, but they would need the whole two weeks to think about the drawing and overhaul it as needed. As it turned out, it was good that they had that time. But in the end, their final picture was completely different from their first sketch (see Figure 2.1).

These students faced a more ambiguous task than the ones who worked on the nine-dot problem. Instead of one possible solution, there were as many solutions as groups of students. Instead of relatively clear guidance about how to begin solving the problem ("Find four lines"), there was vague guidance ("Find any sort of connections"). But the teacher still defined "the" problem, even if she did it indirectly via the instruction sheet. In effect, she said to Jerry, Brendon, and Kalli, "You can choose any connections among words and make any drawing that you

FIGURE 2.1

Jerry, Brendon, and Kalli's Sketch

Preliminary Sketch   Final Sketch

In Your Own Voice

One reviewer of this passage wrote that I sounded too critical of children's creativity, that children and young people *are* creative if only teachers and parents will let them be.

What do you think about this possibility?

If you support it, how would you then distinguish between the creative accomplishments of children and those of adults?

choose, but you *have* to choose something." The students were not really free to *not* do the task.

All things considered, then, does this drawing and free-association task call for creativity? Yes, in that it encourages students to see unique solutions to a problem. No, in that it still does not, any more than the nine-dot activity does, allow students to define or set the problem in the first place. But yes, in that some students may create interesting, pleasing relationships among word meanings. But no, in that other students may create solutions that are merely bizarre or strange. Giving Jerry, Brendan, and Kalli two weeks to create their drawing instead of one day may have encouraged persistence in deciding how to approach the project, and therefore made it more insightful and less bizarre. But there is still no guarantee of a truly creative outcome, one that is not only unusual but also pleasing.

Reconciling the need for something unusual with the need for something pleasing makes it harder to encourage truly creative activity in a classroom—but not impossible! Consider yet another student in another classroom:

Roberta had always *loved* plants. Her parents had encouraged her interest before she ever began grade 3, as her teacher had quickly found out in the first week of school. Roberta had brought Ms. Simon a potted plant as a gift—"something I put together myself, for you," Roberta had said. In free-reading times, and especially during trips to the school library, Roberta sought out books about growing things—houseplants, mostly, "but I also like ecology," she explained when she checked out a large picture book about the rain forest.

So Ms. Simon looked for ways to encourage this interest. "Would you like to enter the city science fair? It's extra work, but I'd give you time now and then. Some of it, though, would have to happen at home."

Roberta asked, "Can I do something on plants?"

"Yes. They want a 'project' or 'experiment.' I can show you the guidelines from the city; it's pretty broad."

Four weeks later, Roberta was immersed in her science fair project, which she was calling "The Effect of Centrifugal Force on Roots." She had gotten the idea from one of the library books on botany: you sprout bean seeds on a record player while it spins for several days and measure which direction the roots grow. Do they grow outward because of the centrifugal force of the turntable or downward because of the earth's gravitation? Day and night the turntable ran in the back of the class while Roberta perfected the technique of sprouting seeds on it successfully. One time they fell off during the night because of the force of the turntable. Another time they dried out and died over the weekend. The third time it worked.

Eight weeks later, Roberta was showing a display of her project in the lobby of her school: a large poster with snapshots of roots growing and text printed in big, bold letters on the school's computer.

Twelve weeks later, Roberta was showing the same display at the science fair, in a big gymnasium with lots of other displays. A judge came by to talk with her. "What did you learn?" he asked.

"That the roots grow down, but sometimes out."

"Hmmm." He smiled.

". . . and that an experiment takes patience—seems like it's easier to describe than to do."

"Really!"

". . . that lima beans work better than mung beans."

A small chuckle from the judge.

". . . that I like growing things."

The judge gave her a good score.

Is Roberta's science project creative? Compared to the threesome who devised connections among random words, Roberta's activity fulfills the criterion of being "pleasing" and not simply unusual or bizarre. A pleasing result was more possible because Roberta chose to do the project—to solve a problem about root growth—herself; and presumably her self-motivation encouraged her persistence, a quality important for a creative outcome. Judged against her own developing knowledge, furthermore, it fulfills the criterion of being unique or unusual: she presumably learned things about roots and scientific experimentation that were entirely new to her.

On balance, then, this example comes closer than the others to representing true creativity. Notice, though, that it also veers back toward focused problem solving, the kind described earlier in this chapter in the work of doctors, managers, lawyers, and psychologists. Creativity and problem solving, it seems, may be similar in important ways, at least when they occur in children and youth. Solutions to problems can be both pleasing and unusual, and therefore creative in the sense I am talking about here. But sometimes solutions can also be expected and boring, the result of well-practiced skills known to all. In the latter case, problem solving may represent talent but not creativity (Feldman, 1986; Sosniak, 1990).

But even this distinction may be misleading. Careful observations of highly creative adults suggest, in particular, that their creative works develop out of a long, slow accumulation of knowledge, skills, and small achievements (Wallace & Gruber, 1992). The artist Picasso practiced painting techniques for years, and most of his practice yielded no masterpieces; Einstein toyed with interesting ideas about the physical universe for an equally long time, but without producing the theory of relativity. The common belief that creative works appear like a bolt of lightning out of nowhere appears to be just a myth. Or, to push the metaphor a bit further: inspirational lightning may sometimes strike, but the lightning itself is really the result of a long, complex build-up of electrical charges and storm formation.

If this interpretation of creativity is true, we should not expect full-blown creativity in the activities or behaviors of young people if what we are looking for are final products and masterpieces. We should instead look for activities that are precursors to full masterpieces, that make "showcase" accomplishments possible later in life. Viewed this way, which of the classroom examples described earlier in this chapter would be the most successful? Which would set the stage for fully creative achievement later, perhaps even months or years later? Would it be the nine-dot problem, the problem of five random words, or Roberta's science fair project? I have commented on their relative merits for promoting creativity in the short term, but what about the long term? A difficult question indeed, but therefore perhaps a good place to end this discussion.

A Conclusion: Thinking Is Various

No matter how much I think about thinking, it seems that I cannot pin it down, cannot identify "universals" that meaningfully explain students' cognitive activity. Instead, various kinds of thinking seem possible. There is scholastic aptitude, the kind of thinking that helps a child answer classroom test questions, but there is also everyday reasoning, the kind that helps her find the best buy in a grocery store. There is problem solving, both the kind that helps a professional find and define a problem in the first place and the kind that allows solutions to self-defined problems. There is creativity, the kind of thinking that creates truly new ideas and products.

Take a closer look at these forms of thinking when you think you see one of them happening. Ask yourself whether the thinking would be easy or difficult to encourage in a classroom, and why. Ask yourself whether the thinking might occur automatically because it fits naturally with the usual circumstances of classroom life or with the usual expectations of students, teachers, and parents. And ask yourself whether the thinking could survive a teacher's efforts to encourage it: would it be the "same" cognitive activity if students were told to do it rather than choosing to do it themselves? When you have begun asking these questions, you will be a step closer toward constructing a useful, unique vision of teaching and learning. You do not need to answer the questions to be a step closer; you just need to ask them.

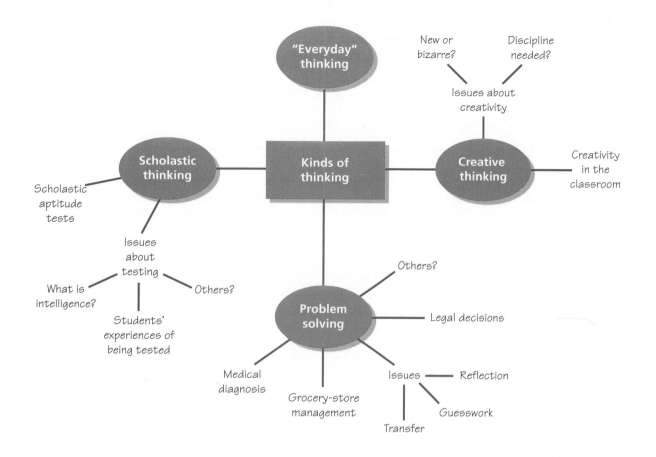

Chapter Re-View: Thinking About Thinking This Chapter Re-View suggests directions in which the chapter might have taken your thinking—though, of course, other directions are also possible. It expands the Chapter View, which suggests a starting point, conceptually, for the chapter. But this Re-View does not suggest an ending point. Like the Chapter View, it represents just one perspective among many.

Key Terms and Concepts

Annotated Readings

Gardner, Howard. (1994). *Creating minds: An anatomy of creativity seen through the lives of Freud, Einstein, Picasso, Stravinsky, Eliot, Graham, and Gandhi*. New York: Basic Books. Howard Gardner has written many readable but thought-provoking books about psychological issues. Here he explores the circumstances that supported creativity in the lives of several renowned creative individuals and, in doing so, reveals clues about the nature of creativity itself and how we might encourage it in ourselves and our students.

Hirsch, E. D. (1996). *The schools we need and why we don't have them*. New York: Doubleday. This is a book I disagree with strongly, but nonetheless it presents an important point of view about education. Hirsch's approach is best described as extremely traditional and "back to basics." At the heart of his viewpoint is an assumption that thinking and learning are at their best in academic settings, but only to the extent that the settings focus on transmitting crucial common content to students.

Perkins, David. (1992). *Smart schools: Better thinking and learning for every child*. New York: Free Press. The information-processing view at its best: a readable account of how to make the cognitive side of schooling as effective as possible. Many sensible suggestions and implications for teaching.

Internet Resources

<www.mensa.org> The web site for Mensa, the international organization for individuals who score in the top 2 percent of the population on standardized tests of intelligence. As you might suppose from this definition of their membership, the web site contains information about and support for a "scholastic" view of intelligence, but also for a more problem-solving view. It provides articles and materials, among other things, as well as a special section about the education of gifted children.

<www.fis.utoronto.ca/~easun/babette> This is a new web site for a group called the Special Interest Group for Arts-Based Methods of Research in Education. The group is a section of a large "umbrella" professional association called the American Educational Research Association. The Arts-Based group is dedicated to finding creative ways to use the arts (such as drama, music, poetry) to communicate the results and interpretations of educational research.

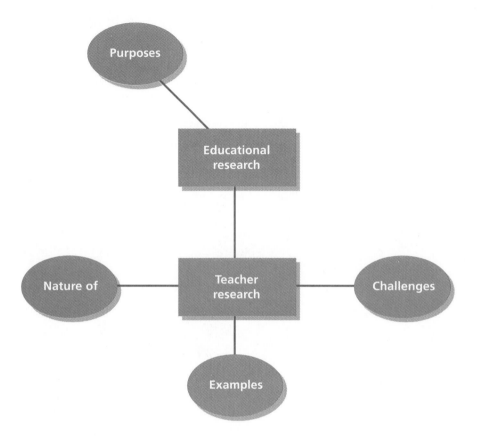

Chapter View: Hearing Distant Voices—Interpreting Teacher Research This Chapter View is a concept map that indicates one among many ways of thinking about the chapter. It suggests a starting point, conceptually, for the chapter but is incomplete by itself. At the end of the chapter is a Chapter Re-View, which expands on the Chapter View, suggesting directions for taking your thinking further—though, of course, other directions are also possible.

3

Hearing Distant Voices: Interpreting Teacher Research

Imagine you are having a dinner party, the purpose of which is to offer you advice and support for your teaching and to answer questions specific to teaching and learning that may be nagging you. You can invite anyone you like, from anywhere on earth and from any time in human history, without regard for practical difficulties and without worrying about whether other people would consider your guests "appropriate." Whom would you invite?

Once you start thinking about it, the possibilities are endless. Of course, you could invite an experienced teacher whom you admired as a child or whom you currently admire; this person would likely have important wisdom to share. But you may have other, less obvious choices as well. Maybe there is a trusted relative whose opinion you would value about an activity as important as teaching (for me it was my grandmother, unfortunately long since deceased). Or maybe there is an author or two who you suspect would understand your world and the challenges you face. Or perhaps a renowned leader of a political or social movement or a religious leader you have known or would like to have known. Never mind whether all your guests speak the same language; we will assume they have all learned English just to attend your dinner

In Your Own Voice

If *you* designed your dinner, of course, you might prefer a different mix of people than the one suggested here.

Who would be in your particular group, and why?

party! We will assume, furthermore, that this evening they are all happy to attend to your wish: to discuss general issues and specific problems related to your teaching.

Once your dinner party is assembled, three things could happen. First, and most generally, the guests might comment helpfully on why teaching is a good choice of profession for you given *your* particular circumstances. Initially they might make only general comments about the value of teaching in society and on the nature of teaching and learning as they see it. But you could guide your guests to focus their comments on you: you could tell them of real, personal experiences that shaped your views of teaching and learning, or that motivated you to enter this field. The resulting interplay of ideas would help you develop a way of thinking about teaching. It would "frame" your own ideas about education, give you a perspective for interpreting your ideas and for understanding your place in the educational world.

Second, your guests might offer specific advice about appropriate teaching practices. Maybe you would talk about how you might handle a certain classroom disruption that you recall from your own schooling or that one of your guests recalls from his or her experience. Or you might talk about a challenging curriculum task, such as how to "get through" to certain students about the meaning of a difficult concept in science. The advice might come up in the course of more general advice and reflection, such as that just mentioned, but it would have a more practical flavor: here is how I would do this; how would you do it?

Third, you might sometimes find your guests persuading you of the importance of certain actions related to teaching. "You have got to know your students personally," one might say; or "You have got to get your parents comfortable with talking with you and visiting their children's classroom"; or "It is important for you to include *all* students in your class, even the ones with special needs." The immediate focus in these comments would not be on *how* to do these things (that too might happen, but at other points in the dinner party). The focus would be on the *rightness* or *desirability* of the actions and on getting you or others to agree about their rightness. As with your guests' specific advice, their persuasive comments would likely be interspersed with their general advice and perspective taking. If your dinner is a long, leisurely one, there will be time for it all: time for framing, offering practical advice, and persuading.

Three Purposes of Educational Research

*W*HOEVER your particular dinner guests would be, the resulting conversation would share purposes intended by **educational research,** or the systematic study of educational problems. First, both the dinner and educational research *provide a framework for thinking about teaching and learning* (Hittleman & Simon, 1997; Hubbard & Power, 1993). A "framework" in this context means a perspective or general viewpoint for understanding specific events and actions—including, in this case, the events and actions related to teaching and learning. Second, both the dinner and educational research *offer advice to be applied to appropriate teaching practices:* How might I initiate reading instruction to first-graders? What could I do on the first day? What if I were initiating reading instead with a fourth-grader who's been having learning difficulties? Or what if I were teaching a course in literacy to adult learners? Educational research exists that has tried to answer these questions and others with a similarly practical slant. Third, both the dinner and educational research *advocate ideas and persuade others* to take actions benefiting students and society. Is it a good or a bad idea to retain (or hold back) a student in grade level for another year if the student fails the curriculum the first time? Some educational research makes recommendations about this sort of a question, in this case retention in grade. But since the recommendations may not coincide with all teachers' initial beliefs, the authors of the research may make an effort not just to present their findings but to persuade their readers or audience of the merits of their recommendations. Note that opening yourself to people whom you respect does not mean giving up thinking for yourself about education. At our imaginary dinner party, you are seeking others' opinions precisely to develop and clarify your own views and distinguish them from others'.

At its best and when properly understood, educational research creates an analogous relationship between others' ideas and your own. It provides general perspectives about teaching and learning, recommends appropriate teaching practices, and persuades educators and members of the public that certain educational practices are desirable. Yet doing so does *not* mean you cannot or should not think about these matters for yourself. On the contrary—and like your dinner party—educational research is meant to stimulate your own knowledge and beliefs: it should create rather than undermine your individuality as a teacher. Authors of research articles are like the guests at the dinner party: each has poten-

In Your Own Voice

If you could immediately, today, get access to any educational research at all, what topic or problem would you want it to tackle?

Would it be about classroom management, as suggested here, or about some other topic?

tial contributions to make, but none has final answers. Not all of the guests' contributions will be equally helpful; some comments may be true and useful, but not for you at this time. If you are just now starting as a teacher, for example, you may be especially interested in anything said about classroom management but less interested in the problems of administering schools or of the political issues that always accompany the educational enterprise. Your dinner guests may talk about both sorts of issues anyway, and your job will be to sort out their more useful comments from their less immediately useful ones.

To experience educational research in this way, however, you must read the authors of research literature as if they were collaborators as well as authorities. You must think of their printed comments as part of a dialogue about teaching and learning that may include you if you choose to participate in it. There are several strategies for adopting this attitude—more, in fact, than we have space to discuss. To keep the discussion short enough, we will focus on just two strategies for hearing the voices of educational research. One strategy is to understand the **purposes** of any particular piece of research that you encounter in order to assess its current usefulness to your daily work and your long-term professional goals. The other strategy is to begin thinking about whether—and how—you, as a teacher, can contribute to the purposes of educational research by creating your own *teacher research*.

Why Was This Research Published?

*M*ost published studies on teaching do not address every purpose of educational research equally. Instead they emphasize only one of the major purposes: either providing a framework, specifying teaching practices, or advocating educational ideas (Floden & Buchmann, 1990). The emphasis of a particular publication affects its style, content, and significance in ways that are both obvious and subtle. The effects in turn influence how a reader, including yourself, should interpret or understand the research. Let's look briefly at the differences in style, content, and significance, and then at their impact on you as a developing, reflective teacher interested in gathering information and ideas about teaching. In the next section, we'll consider several examples of educational research, each chosen because it emphasizes a different mix of purposes and therefore calls for different interpretations and responses from readers.

First, the major purpose of a research article affects how completely the research tries to create *universal truths as opposed to truths that are local or dependent on circumstances.* If the purpose is to give you a perspective on how students learn *in general,* for example, the research may gloss over or tend to ignore obvious differences in how students learn in the interest of being relevant to as many learning situations as possible. In reading this sort of research, your job is to make allowances (mentally) for this fact given what you already know from experience, reflection, and other reading about students' learning. You must ask yourself whether the circumstances of your students and classroom dilute the relevance of a general "perspective" piece of research. This will be challenging if you lack experience and are too new at teaching to have done much reading of research—though you should always be able to reflect on the conclusions contained in a research piece. In fact, because of the challenges of evaluating the adequacy of general claims about teaching and learning, you may initially prefer to read research that focuses more directly on classroom teaching practices. This choice may be fine, but it may also limit how quickly or completely you can develop a perspective of your own; the "framing" perspectives contained in some research studies can help you to do so.

In any case, the second difference that the purpose of the research makes is by influencing the **response that an author expects** from you, the reader: does he or she expect you to actually do something new or simply to consider doing something new? Or even just to be aware of a new idea? Advocacy research, for example, may deliberately sound as though it expects action. If it is about the benefits and problems of including students with special needs in regular classes, for example, you may take a moral position: you should include these students, it may seem to say. A teaching practice article, on the other hand, may merely ask you to consider alternatives to your normal ways of teaching: certain strategies worked here (in the research you just read about), it says, so think about whether they might work for you as well.

Less obviously, any piece of published research will make unstated **assumptions about prior experiences and attitudes** of its readers. A framework piece may assume, for example, that you are already familiar with theories of learning, although if it truly is educational research, it may primarily assume familiarity with everyday classroom applications of the theories. Therefore, an education-oriented study to assess the behaviorist concept of reinforcement may be relatively accessible to you even if you never made a career of studying the theoretical details of behaviorist theory. It might seem more accessible than you expect because, for

In Your Own Voice

As you read this book, what experiences and beliefs does it seem that I, Kelvin Seifert, am expecting from you, the reader?

(And are they reasonable?)

example, it uses teachers' praise of students' learning, a notion with which you do have some experience, as the chief reinforcement observed in the research.

Similarly, research that focuses on specific teaching practices or on moral advocacy makes assumptions about your experiences and attitudes. A teaching practices piece may assume that you have taught a class in the past, or at least that you are familiar enough with classroom life to understand discussions of teaching practices. The idea of "withitness" (keeping track of multiple activities), for example, originated from observations of teachers managing large-group classroom activities; but even if you have not yet begun your teaching career, it is possible to understand the idea and its potential value when you eventually do teach. An advocacy piece of research, on the other hand, may assume you do in fact enjoy persuading others of your point of view, even when others initially disagree or react indifferently. The assumptions may show up as much in what the writing omits as in what it explains: if the term *cooperative learning activity* is used without explanation, for example, the researcher may be assuming you are the sort of person—perhaps a teacher—who already knows what that term means and therefore believe in the value of cooperative learning.

Having made these distinctions, I must qualify them by saying that an individual research study or publication rarely serves *only* one purpose at a time; it merely emphasizes one purpose more than others. A study that offers a theoretical framework may also use its framework to suggest specific teaching practices or to advocate new ways to organize education to benefit students. And vice versa: a study that describes new, effective teaching practices may as a result suggest, or at least imply, a new way to understand students' learning in general or new actions that educators in general should take. In these ways, research studies are like the guests at the dinner party discussed at the beginning of the chapter: although each person may contribute primarily to one area of your thinking, each is likely to have useful things to say about other areas as well.

Let me illustrate these ideas about the purposes and effects of research by describing and commenting on several examples of actual research studies relevant to education—studies that I found meaningful in some way. The studies are not a full cross-section of educational research, but highlight a particular kind of investigation, those in which teachers take an active role in designing questions and interpreting results. Each example serves a mixture of purposes, but with an emphasis on one of the particular purposes (perspective taking, teaching recommendations, or advocacy) described earlier. The differences in purpose reflect the assumptions the authors of the studies make about their readers and about the mental work the authors hope readers do and the motivations they hope readers will acquire.

The Nature of Teacher Research

In Your Own Voice

Teacher research is sometimes also called *classroom research* and sometimes also *action research*.

Can you think of advantages (or drawbacks) to each of these alternative names?

In view of the purposes of educational research, a particularly important kind of investigation for teachers is called **teacher research,** systematic and intentional inquiry by teachers (Stenhouse, 1985). Teacher research is not to be confused with "research about teaching," which consists of investigations by professional researchers of the topic of teachers or teaching. Teacher research has several defining characteristics. First, it originates in the problems and dilemmas of classroom practice, such as a gap between what a teacher is doing and what she or he would like to be doing, or a chronic problem with certain students, materials, or activities. Second, its outcomes offer information about teachers in particular classroom contexts rather than about teachers in general or students in general. Skeptics argue that this feature makes teacher research less useful than research with a more general focus, but its supporters point out that focusing on particular people and settings makes teacher research more valid simply because it is more attuned to differences among classrooms, teachers, and students. Third, although the audience for teacher research can certainly include professors and educational administrators, it tends to be other teachers (Fenstermacher, 1994). Teacher research is therefore in a stronger position than other research to provide an "insider's" perspective on the problems of teaching (Cochran-Smith & Lytle, 1993).

"It's like that joke," thought Howie after finishing the page above. Julia winced slightly, knowing she couldn't stop him from telling it:

This person is looking for his car keys under a street light at night. So a second person walks up, see? And the second one says, "Did you lose something?"

    "Yeah, my car keys."

    "Under this street light?'"

    "No, way over there," said the first man, pointing out into the darkness.

    "So why are you looking over here?"

    "Because this is where the light is!"

Educational research is sometimes criticized for being like the person in Howie's joke: looking where there is already the "light" of information and theories rather than where the most important educational problems are. But the criticism is not entirely fair. It is true that research studies tend to build on one other and, in this sense, gravitate to where the "light" of previous research and previous thinking already exists. The studies by Saltzstein, Jiménez, and Lipsky/Gartner all cited previous research studies, previous theories, or both as justifications for the problems they addressed. But it is also true that the previous research those three studies cited was based on lasting, important problems of human development and of education. Moral development, bilingual literacy, and inclusive education are all important concerns of teachers and educators, whether or not research has been done about them. The reason later studies gravitate around certain topics, in other words, may have as much to do with the importance of the topic as with the fact that others have already studied it.

From a teacher's point of view, it might be more accurate to say that the problem with a lot of educational research is lack of access to the most appropriate examples of it at the most helpful times. If I am teaching first-grade mathematics for the first time, for example, I need the benefit of research on *this* topic, not on some other educational topic, and I need it *now*, not at some later time in my career. How am I to locate that research? And even if I do find it, how can I be sure I am understanding the special language and research procedures often embodied in many educational research studies? These problems are not impossible to solve, but they do require becoming familiar with the research literature in general, much as you can begin finding books in the public library more easily after you start visiting the library regularly and get to know how it is organized. Interpreting research studies, furthermore, is a skill in itself, one that takes time to acquire and often benefits from guidance by others who already have some of it. It is a professional challenge to acquire skill at finding and interpreting educational research, but far from an impossible one.

Teacher research offers one way to begin meeting that challenge, because it begins with problems of classroom practice and therefore stimulates you (as a teacher) both to observe your own students and to search for published educational research about particular problems of high concern to you. In a sense, it transforms Howie's joke about the man looking for car keys under the light rather than where the keys actually are. With teacher research, the joke should now be told like this:

"That's *so* ancient, Howie," Julia said disdainfully. "I've heard it before, and I bet some of the other readers have too."

"So? So tell a better one." Howie was annoyed, but was willing to listen.

A teacher is sitting outside in the dark with a flashlight in her lap.

In Your Own Voice

I use a flashlight analogy here, but this too may be misleading because it implies that you do your teacher research alone and that you focus your attention into a narrow "beam."

Do you think these assumptions are accurate?

If not, can you think of a better analogy for explaining the nature of teacher research?

Another teacher comes up and asks, "Why are you sitting in the dark like this?"

"I'm looking for something," says the teacher.

"But you're just sitting there, not even using your flashlight!"

"I know," she says. "First, I have to decide what to look for."

Perhaps, suggest some educators, educational research should be more like this teacher's search: before you can begin, you have to figure out what you are looking for. In that case, when you do begin to search, maybe you will need only a small light—a flashlight—as long as the light is portable and can shine where you really need it.

Teacher Research in Practice

Teacher research has a number of features in addition to the defining ones already mentioned (Richardson, 1994). To varying degrees, most such studies support some combination of these ideas:

1. Teaching is really a form of research.
2. Teacher research, like teaching itself, requires substantial reflection.
3. Collaboration among teachers is crucial for making teacher research meaningful and for the improvement of teaching.
4. Teachers' knowledge of teaching has to be shared publicly, especially when gained systematically through teacher research.

To see how these features look in practice, let's look at several examples of teacher research studies.

Example: Focusing on Motivating Students

In 1993, Patricia Clifford and Sharon Friesen published an account of their effort to develop a classroom program based on students' outside interests and experiences. Clifford and Friesen were co-teachers in a double-size classroom that deliberately included children from first, second, and third grades.

Because of prior experiences, the teachers were led to their research by three major questions, which they phrased like this:

- *How can a curriculum remain open to children's unique experiences and connect with the world they know outside the school?* The teachers believed that all too often the official school curriculum lacked meaning for children because it seemed cut off from the rest of the world. The result was unmotivated students and poor learning.

- *Why is imaginative experience the best starting point for planning?* The teachers believed that imaginative experiences—make-believe play, stories, poems—provided access to children's lives outside school. Perhaps somehow these could be connected to the goals of the official curriculum.

- *What happens when teachers break down the barriers between school knowledge and real knowledge?* In drawing on children's outside experiences, would children actually become more or less motivated? Would children take over the program and fail to learn the official curriculum goals?

To answer these questions, the teachers kept extensive diaries or journals for one entire school year. In the journals, they described and reflected on their daily teaching experiences. The teachers also talked with each other extensively about classroom events and their significance, and the results of the conversations often made their way into the journals. For example, the teachers recorded in their journals an experience with students about ways of telling time. In preliminary discussions, the students became interested in how a sundial works. So the teachers and students went outside and created a human sundial using the students themselves. The teachers' journal chronicled these events, and noted the comments and questions students developed as a result:

- If you stood in the same place for a whole day you would see your shadow change places because the earth changes position.

- Why is my shadow longer than I am in the evening, but shorter at noon?

- Clouds can block the sun's rays, so sundials won't work on rainy days.

- How did people start to tell time?

As the year evolved and observations accumulated and were recorded, the teachers gradually began to answer their own three questions. They found, for example, that connecting the curriculum with children's interests and motives was most effective when they could establish a personal bond with a child. They also found that imaginative expression helped certain children to feel safe to explore ideas. And they found that blending school knowledge and "real" knowledge caused children to learn much *more* than before, although much of the additional knowledge was not part of the official curriculum. With these conclusions in mind, and with numerous examples to support them, Clifford and Friesen published their study so that others could share what they had learned about teaching, learning, and students.

In Your Own Voice

If you were a teacher reading the study by Clifford and Friesen, how would you make allowances for the differences in circumstances between your own students and your own teaching compared to the students and teaching goals described in their article?

How might you avoid overgeneralizing from their work to yours while still drawing useful ideas from theirs?

The study by Clifford and Friesen is interesting in its own right, of course, but for our purposes, try stepping aside from its content for a moment and look at the research as an example of teacher research. First, the research incorporated teaching: Clifford and Friesen were teaching while they studied their program, and studied their program while they were teaching. Second, the research required considerable reflection over a long period of time: their journals and conversations contained not only descriptions of events but also their interpretations of the events. Third, the study involved collaboration: not one but two teachers were studying the major questions. Finally, the teachers developed their results and conclusions not only for themselves but also for others. These four qualities make the study by Clifford and Friesen a clear example of teacher research. Note, though, that other studies conducted by teachers may be less clear-cut; they may show some of these four features, but not all, as in the next two examples.

Example: Focusing on Development

In 1986, Vivian Paley published a short book called *Mollie Is Three*, one of a series based on her observations of children as a prekindergarten teacher. Paley was interested in how young children develop or change over the long term, and in particular how the development looks from the point of view of a classroom teacher. She observed one child in particular, Mollie, from the time she entered nursery school just after her third birthday until after she turned four years old. Paley's interest focused not so much on curriculum, as Clifford and Friesen's had, as on Mollie as a whole person; "the subject which I most wished to learn," wrote Paley, "is children" (p. xiv). She therefore wrote extended narrative (or storylike) observations about the whole range of activities of this one child, and included periodic brief reflections on the observations. Because the observations took a narrative form, the resulting book reads much like a novel: some themes are simply implied by the story line rather than stated explicitly. Using this approach, Paley demonstrated (and occasionally also stated) several important developmental changes. At age three, for example, Mollie's language was often disconnected from her actions: she would talk about one thing but do another. By four, she was much more likely to tie language to her current activities, and in this sense she more often "said what she meant." A result of the change was that Mollie also began understanding and following classroom rules as the year went on, because the language of rules became more connected (in her mind) to the actions to which they referred.

In Your Own Voice

Suppose Vivian Paley had written about children's learning and development not in the form of a story but in the form of an essay.

Would an essay format seem more general and therefore more convincing?

Or would it seem less vivid and therefore less convincing?

Vivian Paley's book had some of the characteristics of teacher research, but had differences as well. Like the research by Clifford and Friesen, Paley's work was based on her teaching and her teaching was based on the research; and once again the research involved periodic reflection on teaching and the public sharing of the reflections. Unlike Clifford and Friesen, though, Paley worked independently, without collaboration. And compared to Clifford and Friesen, she deliberately integrated observation and interpretation as one might do in a piece of fiction to make the "story" imply or show its message without having to tell it in so many words. In this regard, her work resembles what some educators have called **arts-based research,** studies that take advantage of an artistic medium (in this case, narrative writing) to heighten readers' understanding and response to research findings (Barone & Eisner, in press). If you are studying the use of space in the classroom, for example, photographs, drawings, or scale models of the room may be especially helpful in strengthening your conclusions. If you are studying children's musical knowledge, on the other hand, recordings of performances by the children may be more appropriate. Of course, you can also write about classroom space or children's music, but both forms of understanding may lose something in "translation" to a written format.

Example: Focusing on Collaboration

In 1996, an example of teacher research was published that was intended for classroom teachers and university researchers at the same time and focused on the challenges of collaboration among educators. Wendy Schoener (a teacher) and Polly Ulichny (a university researcher) jointly published a study in which they explored how, or even whether, teachers and university researchers could participate as equals in the study of teaching (Ulichny & Schoener, 1996). Wendy (the two used their first names throughout their published study) was a teacher of adults learning English as a second language (ESL); Polly was a specialist in multicultural education and wanted to observe a teacher who was especially successful at reaching the ethnically diverse students who normally study ESL. Polly therefore asked Wendy for permission to study her teaching for an extended period of time: to visit her class, videotape it, interview her about it, and the like.

What followed is best described as an extended "negotiation" between teacher and professor for access to Wendy's class on the one hand and for mutual respect for each other's work on the other. In the published article, the negotiations are described separately by each participant to honor the differences in their concerns and perspectives. Before, during, and after the observations, Polly and Wendy each had to adjust her expectations of what the other could do and was willing to do. As the authors put it, some things were "easy to hear" from the other and some things were "hard to hear." Wendy, as a teacher, found it easier to hear criticisms of her teaching if they came from herself rather than from the higher-status university professor, Polly. Polly, for her part, found it easier to hear Wendy's self-criticisms if she matched Wendy's self-evaluations and disclosures with some of her own; Polly began telling about dilemmas and problems she experienced in her own (university) teaching. Because of tendencies such as these, the two educators eventually focused less on Polly's original purpose—studying multicultural teaching—and more on the problem of how teachers and university researchers might collaborate effectively.

Overall, this study qualifies as a piece of teacher research, but it can also be considered an example of research *about* teaching. Consider the criterion described earlier: the study meets them, but always ambiguously. First, the research did involve collaborative reflection by the participants, but the reflection was only partly about classroom teaching; the rest was about how the relationship between Wendy and Polly developed. Second, the research observations did focus on classroom teaching—Wendy's teaching; however, they originated not with Wendy's concerns about her own classroom but with Polly's need to study multicultural teaching. Third, the researchers did share what they learned by publishing their observations and ideas, but their article speaks not only to teachers but also to university researchers and educators of future teachers. Their dual audience is understandable given their focus on the relations between these two communities. But it makes the study less clearly a piece of *teacher* research as such.

In pointing out these differences, I am *not* implying praise for pure, "politically correct" examples of teacher research or criticism for mixed or "impure" examples. Quite the contrary: the point is to notice how diverse studies by teachers can be and to appreciate the diversity. Whatever their specific features, classroom studies by teachers hold in common a commitment to giving a voice to teachers as they reflect on their work, and reflect especially on problems and challenges intrinsic to classroom life. This goal can be accomplished through more than one method: through journals and other recordkeeping methods, through oral discussions with colleagues, and through written reflections created either for themselves or for others concerned about teaching and learning. The diversity of topics and methods should not surprise us, in fact, since students, teachers, and classrooms are themselves so diverse.

In Your Own Voice

Suppose Wendy and Polly had been two teachers instead of a teacher and a university researcher.

What would be gained by this difference, and what would be lost?

Or suppose both had been university researchers.

Could the study have been done at all in that case?

The Challenges of Teacher Research

*W*ELL and good, you may say. Teacher research offers teachers a way to hear one another, to learn from their own and others' experience. But this benefit comes at a cost, both in time and effort, as it did for Wendy (and Polly) described in the previous section. By definition, no one can do teacher research *for* teachers; they must do it for themselves. In fact, given the stresses often experienced when you begin teaching, you may need to satisfy yourself at first with appreciating other teachers' classroom-based research, whether you see it in writing or hear about and discuss it orally. Sooner or later, though, you will need to confront the fact that other teachers inevitably study problems and dilemmas that occur in other classrooms, and that these may not coincide with the ones you experience with your own students. Ultimately, the only solution to this problem is to initiate teacher research of your own, focusing on classroom challenges unique to yourself. Your projects need not be as long term or comprehensive as the ones described in this chapter, but they will need to be systematic and reflective.

Doing your own teacher research raises several important questions. First, how do you know what, from all of your experiences, deserves special study and reflection? Second, is teacher research practical for the circumstances, or will it detract from your teaching and from students' learning? Third, will others, especially principals and teachers, support your engagement with teacher research, and perhaps even try to help create conditions that support doing such research? These questions do not have simple or definitive answers, but let's consider briefly how you might begin answering them for yourself.

In Your Own Voice

What topic or problem might be worthy of study for *you* if you were a teacher researcher?

Would it be the same topic or problem that you identified on page 59 in connection with "conventional" educational research?

What Is Worthy of Study?

Since this question has moral overtones, it is indeed complex. But a brief, preliminary answer is easy to give: teachers should study either what intrigues them the most about their work or what troubles them the most. But only you can decide which features or issues deserve priority in your particular case, and therefore might merit some form of classroom research. How can you decide what your priorities actually are? Try reflecting on your work frequently, and try discussing it with other educators or other individuals whom you trust. In a way, this is the major advice underlying this primer.

Is Teacher Research Practical?

From one perspective, the answer has to be "Of course not!" Teacher research is not practical because it takes time and effort that presumably could be used in some other way. Viewed very generally, however, teaching itself is not "practical" in one sense: it takes time and effort to implement any sort of classroom program, and the resulting work often is labor intensive. Teaching students always takes a lot of work. Since systematic reflection on teaching (i.e., classroom-based research) is also work, the question should be whether time invested in reflection improves your effectiveness as a teacher and students' effectiveness as learners. If it does, teacher research is "practical."

Looked at in this way, teacher reseach is indeed practical, though perhaps not in every way on every occasion. If you choose to learn about the quality of conversational exchanges between yourself and students, for example, you will need some way to record these dialogues, or at least to keep accurate, detailed notes on them. Doing so may or may not be practical, depending on your circumstances. On the other hand, if you choose to study how and why certain students remain on the margins of your class socially, this problem too may or may not be practical as a topic for teacher research, depending on whether you can find a way to observe and reflect on students' social interactions or lack thereof. It all depends on your circumstances: on the attention you can afford to divert to your problem and the demands placed on you as a teacher in relation to the benefits that solutions to the problems will give you.

Nonetheless, educators continually debate the potential of teacher research. Some argue that the nature of teaching is inherently incompatible with the nature of research (Wong, 1995); hence the two cannot be combined. Teaching calls for action, choice, and decision: classes need materials, students need ideas, and programs need choices in order to function. Research calls for understanding and observation: from this perspective classes need to be observed, students and teachers need to be interviewed, and programs need to be analyzed. The two sets of activities, it is argued, are incompatible. One set is done at the expense of the other.

Other educators argue that the dilemma is illusory. This is the view expressed by Yvette Daniel, a high school English teacher, in the accompanying Multiple Voices box. As Ms. Daniel implies, teaching and research conflict only if you define both activities narrowly; with broader definitions, they become compatible. For example, teaching involves more than the interactions with students that take place during class ses-

In Your Own Voice

It seems that not all educational problems are equally easy to study.

Is there one that you might have information about but might be especially difficult to study, either as conventional research or as teacher research?

In essence, Kelvin asks here whether teaching interferes with research. Some might argue that it does, that there is a great divide between teaching and research. This happens, I think, because we tend to think of research in terms of surveys and statistics, and not as something engaging and self-renewing. The verbs used to represent teaching are *act, choose,* and *decide* as opposed to *understand* and *observe* for research. In my opinion, though, the "chasm" is irrelevant and artificial. Empirical inquiry should not be viewed as a separate entity with goals different from teaching. As a teacher, my choices and decisions are based for the most part on my understanding and observations of my students—which are essentially research activities. Observing the subtleties and nuances of students' behavior is the key, and this can often be done best by a teacher who knows the students on a daily basis.

Yvette Daniel, High School English Teacher, Toronto, Ontario, Canada

sions; it also includes preparations and planning times before and after class sessions. If these are included, teacher research is always possible; that is, teachers can always reflect on the events of the day (Wilson, 1995). Research, for its part, is more than passive observation of students and classrooms; it also includes educational interventions, efforts to stimulate students to new thinking and new responses. Even under these broader definitions, of course, some classroom studies are ruled out as impractical or even unethical. You cannot prolong dialogues excessively, for example, or deliberately teach incorrect information to students "just to see if they notice." But some investigations are impossible for *any* form of research. In medical research, for example, you cannot investigate a medical treatment that is extremely painful or deliberately withhold a drug of proven value "just to see what happens."

Will Others Support Your Teacher Research?

Since teacher research is tied closely to teaching itself, both critics and supporters agree that success with teacher research means challenging traditional beliefs and practices about the conduct of teaching (Eisner, 1991). The reflectiveness called for by teacher research in particular means less time working alone than is customary and more time working with colleagues who support your work and who might even be potential collaborators. To sustain a commitment to classroom inquiry, in other words, you will need people with whom to share teaching experiences, problems, and ideas. The number of such individuals need not be large; in the studies described earlier in this chapter, each teacher had only one collaborator. But they must be supportive so that you can trust them with information about your difficulties as well as your joys and be willing to listen carefully to theirs. They need not, however, agree with everything you do or believe; in fact, both you and your supporters may learn more if you *disagree* sometimes about the significance of particular educational goals or classroom experiences. And a supportive colleague need not actually be another classroom teacher. The study by Polly and Wendy involved a collaboration between a teacher and a university researcher. You may find helpful others where you do not first expect them, such as among the administrators of your school or among teachers at other schools.

Benefiting from All Kinds of Research

WHETHER you, as a classroom teacher, actually undertake teacher research or simply interpret others' research projects, the challenge is to see the value in *all* forms of research, without being tempted to think that only a few, or even only one, can provide useful guidance for teaching (Eisner, 1996; Phillips, 1992). If you can do this, your ways of learning about teaching will be enriched. You will have more ways to understand life in classrooms empathically, but also have some of the benefit of objective distance. You will have more ways to grasp the individuality of particular students, but also to see what they have in common. And you will have more ways to interpret your own experiences as a teacher, but also be able to learn from the experiences of others. Realizing these benefits fully is a challenge, because the very diversity of teaching and learning makes educational problems and solutions diverse as well. But you will also have plentiful company in searching for better understanding, and your company will include both professional researchers and classroom teachers. To the extent that you succeed, you yourself will grow as a professional—a change which I discuss further in the next chapter.

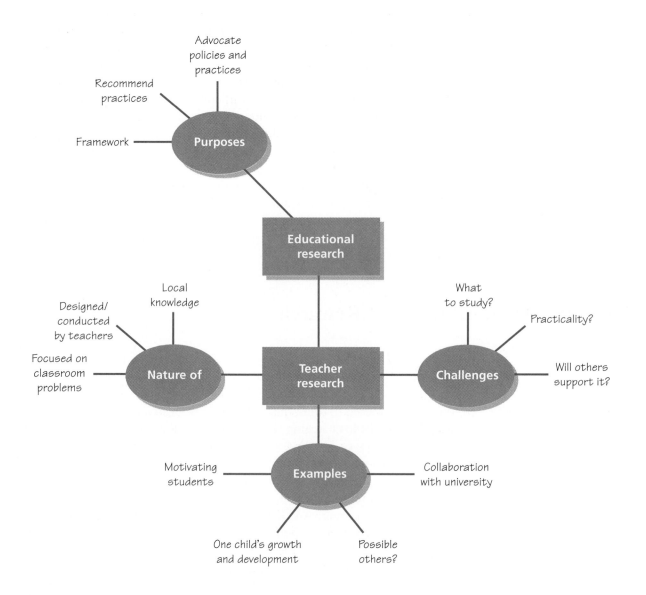

Chapter Re-View: Hearing Distant Voices—Interpreting Teacher Research This Chapter Re-View suggests directions in which the chapter might have taken your thinking—though, of course, other directions are also possible. It expands the Chapter View, which suggests a starting point, conceptually, for the chapter. But this Re-View does not suggest an ending point. Like the Chapter View, it represents just one perspective among many.

Key Terms and Concepts

educational research (59)
purposes of educational
    research (59)
responses expected in reading
    research (61)
assumptions about readers'
    experience (61)
teacher research (63)
arts-based research (68)

Annotated Readings

Anderson, G., Herr, K., & Nihlen, A. (1994). *Studying your own school: An educator's guide to qualitative practitioner research.* Thousand Oaks, CA: Corwin Press.

Hubbard, R., & Power, B. (1993). *The art of classroom inquiry: A handbook for teacher-researchers.* Portsmouth, NH: Heinemann.

McKernan, James. (1996). *Curriculum action research: A handbook of methods and resources for the reflective practitioner* (2nd ed.). London: Kogan Page. As their titles imply, these books offer guidance for conducting classroom-based research. They make good resources for getting started.

Jaeger, R. (Ed.). (1997). *Complementary methods for research in education* (2nd ed.). Washington, DC: American Educational Research Association. This book offers a chapter on each of the major forms of educational research. Each chapter is written by a different authority on educational research, and is both authoritative and accessible in its language. Overall, the book offers a good way to gain perspective on the place of teacher research in the larger landscape of educational research.

Internet Resources

<www.aera.net> This is the official web site of the American Educational Research Association, one of the major "umbrella" professional associations sponsoring educational research in the United States and, indeed, in the entire English-speaking world. The opening page has links to an assortment of divisions and special-interest groups, each specializing in some form of educational research. One special-interest group is called "teacher as researcher"; another is called "arts-based research in education."

<www.ed.gov/offices/OERI> This is the web site of the United States Office of Educational Research and Improvement. It summarizes current research initiatives and programs sponsored by the U.S. federal government, and includes links for finding more information about individual initiatives and programs.

CHAPTER VIEW

```
┌─────────────────────────┐
│   Challenges in becoming │
│   an accomplished teacher│
└─────────────────────────┘
            │
            │
            │
            │
            │
┌─────────────────────────┐
│  Your resources for becoming│
│   an accomplished teacher│
└─────────────────────────┘
```

Chapter View: Looking Ahead This Chapter View is a concept map that indicates one among many ways of thinking about the chapter. It suggests a starting point, conceptually, for the chapter but is incomplete by itself. At the end of the chapter is a Chapter Re-View, which expands on the Chapter View, suggesting directions for taking your thinking further—though, of course, other directions are also possible.

4

Looking Ahead: Developing as a Professional

Education is everything. The peach was once a bitter almond, and the cauliflower is nothing but a cabbage with a college education.

Mark Twain (1899)

Bitter almonds to peaches, and cabbages to cauliflowers? Is that what teaching is all about? And suppose it is; suppose teaching is a process of transforming students, of sculpting the elegant and useful from the everyday. Consider what this might mean for your future as a teacher. What will teaching feel like when you begin? Suppose you have found a teaching position (a challenge in itself!) and face the prospect of educating students. You may be expecting to see as few as twenty each day or as many as a hundred. You may be expecting to hear languages from some students that you cannot understand and to discover special educational needs in some that you can only guess at now. As a newcomer to teaching, you are comparatively unfamiliar with the curriculum the school authorities expect you to implement; how, you wonder, can anyone fill an entire semester or school year with the curriculum, let alone motivate and excite students with it?

The worries are daunting, but they are balanced by other thoughts that are less stressful and more hopeful. You may remember experiences from your past with children or youth: times when you got along wonderfully with them, times that started you thinking about teaching as a career. Or you may remember teachers—not only the ones whose methods you want to avoid but also the ones whom you admired. Or you may remember courses or topics that caught your imagination: subjects that seem especially worthwhile, especially worth sharing with others. The positive memories sustain you while you look ahead to the stresses. Teaching, it appears, will be challenging, but it will be worth the challenge. You are inclined to agree with Mark Twain: education is indeed everything, and you may indeed be able to create some peaches and cauliflowers.

This chapter invites you to look ahead at the challenges and to consider how you may want to grow to become a teacher who is not just good but truly excellent. I cannot know exactly what concerns will be uppermost in your particular mind, of course, but I can suggest challenges for you to consider that other new teachers, and veterans as well, have encountered. I can also suggest strengths and resources that you may already have, or can soon acquire, for addressing your concerns and moving yourself closer to the kind of teacher you want to become. In naming them as challenges, I have been guided mostly by knowledge about life in classrooms, both my own and other educators'. The importance of the challenges to you, though, will depend on your particular history and circumstances. Not everyone needs to grow in the same way or has access to the same supports. In reading this chapter, then, ask yourself these questions: What are the challenges that I feel I must meet to teach well? What strategies will I need to use to meet the challenges?

These two questions, and the reflections they lead to, are familiar to teachers who strive for excellence in their work. They are also familiar to government agencies and educational researchers and writers who have considered what it means to teach well (Sizer, 1996; Strange, 1997; Task Force on Teaching as a Profession, 1986). The agencies and researchers often frame the problem as one of identifying **professional teaching standards,** the qualities and complex skills needed for the finest possible teaching. In effect, professional teaching standards are long-term challenging goals for teachers. They identify levels of performance that not every teacher can attain easily but nonetheless are attainable given time, experience, and dedication to students' learning. Professional teaching standards, therefore, should not be confused with standards for teacher certification, which refer to minimal legal qualifications (often expressed as a set of university credits) required to begin a career as a teacher. Professional teaching standards refer to performance that is not minimal but maximal.

One prominent statement of professional teaching standards has been published by the National Board for Professional Teaching Standards

In Your Own Voice

Before reading the next section, stop and think about your own strengths as a potential teacher.

What do you consider your best quality or skill?

What, on the other hand, do you think you will need to develop further as you gain experience?

Keep your reflections in mind as you read the next section.

(1997), a coalition of nonprofit foundations and professional associations related to education. Relying primarily on advice from classroom teachers themselves, the board proposed several ideas that describe highly accomplished teaching, presented as five propositions. The propositions are listed in Table 4.1. They make a useful framework for considering where you need to develop as a teacher in the years ahead and which aspects of teaching you may find especially challenging. They also help in assessing what skills and qualities you already have that can contribute to your own excellence in this profession. In the next part of the chapter, therefore, I explain some of the thinking behind each proposition, rephrasing it as a challenge to develop in your own work with students. You may find that you do not feel as well prepared in some areas as you would like—though, by the same token, you may also believe you have already made a good beginning toward excellence in other areas. As the discussion unfolds, and especially in the final part of the chapter, we look at how you might find ways to grow where you think you need it and why you can expect to succeed at doing so.

What Will Challenge You About Teaching?

Becoming Committed to Students and Their Learning

In many ways, commitment to students and their learning is the "bottom line" of excellent teaching; without it, there is no point in even having a teaching career. Yet it is not a specific, identifiable skill acquired

TABLE 4.1 Five Propositions of Accomplished Teaching

Proposition 1:	Teachers are committed to students and their learning.
Proposition 2:	Teachers know the subjects they teach and how to teach those subjects to students.
Proposition 3:	Teachers are responsible for managing and monitoring student learning.
Proposition 4:	Teachers think systematically about their practice and learn from experience.
Proposition 5:	Teachers are members of learning communities.

Source: National Board for Professional Teaching Standards, 1997.

One challenge in becoming a professional teacher is to know your subject well. Reaching this goal is a never-ending task: there is always more to be learned. But it is still possible to know your subject well enough to get started as a teacher.
© Elizabeth Crews

Another challenge in becoming a professional teacher is to support, and be supported by, the knowledge of other teachers. Becoming part of a learning community of teachers can help in meeting other goals, such as learning more about the subject you teach.
© Elizabeth Crews

once and for all so much as an attitude that develops over time, eventually permeates all aspects of excellent teaching, and calls for constant renewal with each group of new students. The intangibility can be troubling, as it is for Brieanne Edgeworth, now in her second year of teaching middle school:

After reading the sentences above, Brieanne wondered if *she* was truly committed to teaching, and when she would know if she was. How can I know for sure? she thought. Will I ever know? I sweated bullets last year, surviving that first year of teaching. Surely that counts as commitment! But sometimes then I did question my decision to go into teaching. There were days when the kids frustrated me more than I dared to say. And nights when I couldn't sleep on account of my work: I kept planning and revising the next day in my mind, even though it was 2:00 A.M. and I should have been asleep. Does insomnia show commitment to students, or just show stress?

The fact is that commitment to students and their learning is an ideal, something that teachers develop but never fully reach. What is important, therefore, is not so much being perfectly committed (there will always be times when you are not) as reaffirming commitment and developing it further. Looked at as a process, commitment is accessible no matter how much or how little experience you have. Brieanne has already engaged the process in her first year of teaching, and presumably will continue to do so in her second year and in later years.

As you gain experience, you may keep discovering new evidence that you do indeed care about students. One kind of evidence will be in your growing understanding of how students learn and think, because this knowledge allows you to teach more effectively and to make new knowledge and skills accessible. Knowledge of learning and thinking, combined with commitment to students, can also help you to reconcile students' goals with curricular goals even when the two seem to diverge. Nel Noddings, professor of education at Stanford University, comments in the accompanying "Multiple Voices" on how to handle this dilemma, using math as an example. More generally, knowledge that supports commitment will come from many sources from readings and discussions with others, from your experiences with students, and from your reflections about the experiences, readings, and discussions. But all of this knowledge will be only initial. You must go beyond it by continuing to learn more about students' learning, thinking, and development, and by choosing to use your developing insights helpfully to benefit students.

Commitment to students and their learning can also be seen in the

Two important issues arise here. First, Professor Seifert raises the question, "Knowing that most students have no intention of (for example) becoming professional mathematicians, should the teacher respect and support their nonmathematical priorities or work to create an intrinsic love of mathematics . . . ?" The two goals are not completely incompatible. I would choose to make the first primary and show my respect for the nonmathematical talents of my students. But I would also teach in such a way that these students might, at least occasionally, enjoy math and understand why some people love it as they love, say, art. Working together, we would "get through" as much math as minimally required by the school's standards; but, more important, we would come to respect one another's interests and talents.

The second issue reflects a widespread misunderstanding of what it means to care. Some students do indeed protest that they don't want to be "cared for." But these students, like many of my professional colleagues (who also make such a protest), *do* want people to detect and respond positively to their preferences with respect to styles of human interaction. So they actually do want care! To respond as carer means exactly this: to receive the other and respond as nearly as one can (consistent with your own moral commitments) to what has been received. Caring cannot be done by recipe. It requires sensitivity, flexibility, and a continuing commitment to increase our competence in human relations.

Nel Noddings, Professor, Stanford University

In Your Own Voice

Given these ideas, how committed do you already feel to students and their learning?

Think about what you consider the signs of commitment in yourself—where your interest in students' learning has come from and where you now think it needs to head.

fairness with which you respond to students, regardless of diversity of race, gender, or disability. As with your knowledge and commitment to learning, you are probably already aware of these issues through prior reading, discussion, and experiences. But think of these as taking you only to the doorway of commitment to students and their learning. From this starting point you must carry on by yourself, finding out more about your own students' diversity and actually enacting your beliefs by responding to students with understanding and tolerance.

Finally, commitment to students and their learning can be seen in concern for students' self-esteem, integrity, and healthy participation in the communities to which they belong. These issues include how attitudes of care and commitments to justice develop and can be encouraged in both teachers and students. But they also include the impact of students' social relationships on their classroom learning and how teachers' classroom talk can either empower or silence individual students. Taken together, these issues focus attention on a point so fundamental to teaching that it seems commonplace and easy to forget: that all of our students will someday become adult members of society, whether or not they remember the details of what we teach them. As B. F. Skinner (a behavioral psychologist) once put it, "Education is what is left over after everything else has been forgotten." An excellent teacher's job is to make sure, at the very least, that what "gets left over" in students includes qualities of constructive citizenship.

Knowing Your Subject and How to Teach It

Excellent teachers "know their stuff": they know their subjects well and know how to communicate them to students. The most straightforward way of doing so is to act as a *generous expert,* which refers to enthusiastic, competent sharing of knowledge and of how knowledge is created in the first place. To be a generous expert is to help students think like scientists (if you teach science), or like musicians (if you teach music), or like competent readers (if you teach reading). Michael Collingwood, an experienced high school science teacher, agrees, and also suggests why enthusiasm and generosity with knowledge can be so effective:

MICHAEL: You know how they're always saying that good teachers are enthusiastic? Well, it's true! I think I know why. When I get excited about science, it's like I'm showing my *relationship* to science. It's like science has become an old, respected friend that I'm introducing to new, young friends—to my students. And each time I visit my old friend, I discover something new, as I might with a real friend. The students see that, and like it. It turns science into something more than a lot of concepts and terms; it makes it something you can become connected to. When I'm enthusiastic, students see that science is not just abstractions sitting "out there" in the universe alone, devoid of human contact and relevance. They see that science is something that is known *by* someone, that stands in relationship *to* a human being. I figure that if I am crazy enough to make friends with science, then maybe some of them will be, too!

Another part of knowing your subject and how to teach it involves good instructional management, a key concern for many new teachers. Being an instructional manager means knowing *how* to select and coordinate activities and tasks so that students learn as effectively as possi-

In Your Own Voice

At first glance, it would seem that a high school teacher has *more* need to know his or her subject in depth and *less* need to understand connections between the subject and other subjects.

But is this necessarily true?

Do you agree with this idea or not?

ble. A challenge for excellent teachers is to combine the roles of generous expert and instructional manager: they must know not only know what they teach but how to teach it. The specifics of how to forge this combination will depend on exactly what you are teaching. In early childhood education, for example, it may be especially important to know how a subject relates to *other* fields of knowledge. What skills at drawing contribute to a child's learning to read? How would the connections between drawing and reading alter how each of those subjects are planned and taught by an excellent early childhood teacher? How could the connections be conveyed to students effectively? Maybe they should draw what they read and read what they draw. But how exactly should this happen? Maybe computers could also help: they often have programs both for drawing and for reading. But how exactly should the teacher use the computers? These are all questions related to knowing the subject and how to teach it. Although answering them is beyond the scope of this book, they are normally addressed somewhere in every teacher education program, often in a curriculum or "methods" course.

Monitoring and Managing Students' Learning

Management of activities poses special challenges because of the nature of classrooms, and in particular their unpredictability and complexity. Small wonder that many new teachers rate management as their biggest initial concern and a matter of survival (Jones, 1998; Partin, 1995)! Whether you are new to teaching or a veteran, though, inappropriate behavior by students, either accidental or deliberate, can confuse the sense of order and the purposes you are working toward with your students. Especially as a newcomer to teaching, it is tempting to equate management with self-defense: you may worry too much about how to handle *mis*behaviors and prevent specific disruptions rather than how to orchestrate and coordinate positive, constructive learning. In reality, all teachers do need ways to prevent and eliminate the negatives, but excellent teachers focus much more strongly on creating the positives in the first place (Kohn, 1996). That is how Barbara Fuller, an experienced elementary school teacher, approaches the problem:

BARBARA FULLER: Sometimes in my room it's like there's an "economy of attention," like students can attend to only so many things at a time—so many instructions, or tasks, or attractive classmates, or whatever. More attention to one means less attention to another. So I have to be careful about how much I ask them to keep track of. If they're doing group work, I have to be careful about how much I "drop in" to their discussions; if I do it needlessly, I could distract them from their thinking. If they're all supposed to be listening to me, on the other hand, I have to make it clear that their groups are (temporarily) disbanded; I must remind them that for the moment they do *not* need to consult with working partners about whatever we're studying. A lot of minor misbehavior happens when I forget the human limitations on attention. There can be problems when I forget how hard it can be to listen to two people at once or to talk to one person (like a partner) and listen to another (like me) at the same time. If I can remember about the economy of attention, it's easier to focus *my* attention on arranging positive learning rather than on curing "bad" behaviors.

Hopefully, when you teach, you will be able to focus more on coordinating positive learning than on repairing disruptions. Until you actually meet your students and classes, though, it will be hard to predict how *much* more you can tip the balance toward coordination and away from repair. To some extent, the balance will be influenced by factors beyond your control. Some classes are more prone to disruptions than others, and the reasons are not always clear, especially when the students in them behave well as individuals. And some classes may be harder (or easier) to manage than others, simply because you know less (or more) about the subject or about activities appropriate to it for engaging students. That said, keep in mind that the balance between coordination and repair nonetheless is under your control to some extent. By planning thoroughly before class, for example, you can make disruptions during class less likely—though, of course, not completely absent. Planning does so in two ways. First, it improves your tolerance for the unexpected during class. For example, a discussion that is more (or less) noisy or longer (or shorter) than expected may seem more acceptable if you know that students have focused on crucial goals of the curriculum. Second and more important, good planning tends to ensure that students have constructive things to do—tasks and activities that are incompatible with disruptive behavior. Planning can even lead to forms of participation that eliminate the preconditions leading to disruptions. For example, when learning activities are arranged to take place on students' own time using the Internet, some of the crowding of classroom life may be alleviated, and with it your need to repair classroom disruptions when they occur. This realization, though, is not a good enough reason to use computers; they are not meant simply to keep students out of mischief. Good teachers focus on the positive learning benefits even when using technology in the classroom: "What," asks such a teacher, "will

In Your Own Voice

What kind of balance do you expect will develop when *you* begin teaching?

Think about what is influencing your choice: your students' personalities, the subjects you expect to teach, the working conditions you anticipate, or . . . ?

students gain from using the Internet?" Not "What management problems can I avoid by using it?"

But keeping the right mix of coordination and repair is not the only sort of balance needed to manage a classroom well. Another kind, just as challenging, is discovering combinations of teaching roles that are most appropriate and helpful to students. As indicated earlier, teachers are many things to their students: instructional manager, caring person, and generous expert. These roles are not mutually exclusive, but are expressed in relationship to one another as you teach. The roles develop in the interactions between you and your students. In those contacts and conversations, you must somehow arrange for students to learn (be a manager), you must value and support students' personal qualities and goals (be caring), and you must share enthusiasm and knowledge about what you are teaching (be a generous expert). At any one moment, one of these roles may predominate over another, but in the long term they all play a part in every teaching and learning relationship. Your job as a high-quality teacher is to discover exactly when and where to emphasize each role—as well as additional roles, perhaps, that you will discover as you gain experience.

The more you can focus on orchestrating learning and balancing teaching roles, the more you can attend to monitoring how well students are actually learning. "Monitoring learning" in essence refers to the perennial challenge of assessment and evaluation. Given the diversity of students' backgrounds and the many ways in which learning occurs, it should be no surprise that high-quality assessment requires multiple, complex methods. Conventional paper-and-pencil tests, for example, may be useful as indicators of some forms of learning, but you will probably need additional indicators if you want a full picture of your students' learning. One strategy of broadening information about students' learning is through "authentic" tasks (those related to students' real-world lives and expectations) and portfolios, which deliberately collect a variety of work for assessment and invite students' own comments on it.

Thinking Systematically About Your Practice and Learning from Experience

To teach well, you must gain from your experience; and to gain from experience, you must reflect on it. Self-reflection has been an ongoing theme throughout all chapters of this book; for example, the In Your Own Voice discussions have encouraged it, as have my comments made periodically in the body of the text. Only by questioning your practices can you hope to improve on them. The reason is simple: the best ways to teach are not necessarily the first ones you (or any teacher) try; you must continually consider how else you might have carried out a lesson effectively or what other plans you could have made that might have assisted particular students just as well or better than the ones you actually followed. Maybe you should try the alternatives next time; at any rate, you should keep them in mind.

In addition to daily reflection, it is important to take stock, periodically and deliberately, of general classroom practices and general goals that seem important or that pose chronic problems in your work. If, for example, you are a third-grade elementary teacher, you might ask, "Is there a less abstract way to introduce 'number facts' than what I am now doing?" If you are a tenth-grade math teacher, you might ask, "How can I help students see relationships among mathematical topics so they don't forget each one after it's tested?" If you are a special education teacher, you might ask, "Have I arranged for programs for my students that are truly as challenging and inclusive as possible?" A host of general, reflective questions such as these exist; the ones you choose to think about will depend on your particular teaching concerns and circumstances. Here is a question that had been concerning Karen Dworkin, an upper-elementary teacher for several years:

KAREN DWORKIN: I got interested in a few students who classmates had nicknamed the "bad kids." It seemed to me they were not bad as people, but they sometimes behaved in ways that were difficult to handle. Every year there were always a few students who were inclined to make inappropriate remarks, or crack jokes at the wrong time, or annoy me and others at the wrong times. It was awkward when they did these things. So I started watching these students closely, trying to understand their motives. I kept a journal entirely about "inappropriate remarks," describing incidents and speculating about the reasons behind each of them. It helped! Eventually I had a whole book's worth of descriptions and interpretations about this sort of "bad" behavior. These students' "bad" behaviors, I decided, were really an effort to reassure themselves that they were not powerless and to convince classmates of their power as well. So my job became one of helping the "bad kids" feel competent, socially and academically, without getting drawn into their power games. And I think I'm succeeding, at least with some. I still get kids like that every year, but my journal—or really the thinking and observing behind my journal—helped me not to worry as much as before.

Karen's work verges on being teacher research, a topic discussed in Chapter 3 of this primer, because it was a systematic inquiry by a

In Your Own Voice

What general concerns, as opposed to daily ones, deserve your attention now in looking forward to a career in teaching?

Are they distinct from concerns about daily matters, or are they the same?

teacher into a classroom-based problem. Karen could also have proceeded, however, by consulting published examples of educational research, including studies conducted *for* teachers rather than *by* teachers. As pointed out in Chapter 3, "research" has diverse qualities and purposes: sometimes it provides perspective, sometimes it offers teaching advice, and sometimes it advocates for new practices, among other things. Much educational research is conducted by specialists (usually university professors), but a growing body of it (called "teacher research") is designed and conducted by classroom teachers themselves. Your challenge, as you become an excellent teacher, will not only be to find research on topics that concern you but also to understand the purposes of the studies you find. You must become an intelligent consumer of research. Look for food for thought, but avoid the junk food—the research that does not prove, or is not meant to prove, what it claims.

To the extent that you can indeed think systematically about your teaching, you can serve as a model of an educated person for students as well as colleagues: you will be someone who is curious, intellectually honest, tolerant of differences of opinion, and fair-minded. These qualities are important parts of professional teaching. In fact, they may be the most important parts of that role. As I mentioned earlier, teachers know the content well that they are teaching. But as important as knowledge of content is, it may ultimately matter less than love of learning and the example that love provides for students. Which would you prefer students to take from their contact with you as a teacher: would you prefer that they forgot the content you taught them and pick up qualities of curiosity, intellectual honesty, and fairness, or the other way around? Whenever you play the role of "generous expert," this question will be central if you also wish to be reflective.

Becoming a Member of a Learning Community

Excellent teaching is not a solitary act; it is more like a collaboration with learners and other teachers. In spite of the stereotype of "solitary" teachers working alone in classrooms and unobserved by other adults, the fact is that high-quality teachers consult with others frequently about students' needs and about the best ways to facilitate students' learning. These conversations may be either deliberate or "accidental," but either way they help teachers to improve their teaching. From others you can gain new sources of good information and materials for teaching. You can also find new classroom activities and learn about priorities and values held by others that deserve your consideration.

In Your Own Voice

When you first thought about teaching as a career, how much did you expect to work *with* others?

Do you foresee problems with doing so, and if so, what do you think you should do about them?

Participation in a learning community can happen in various ways. A teacher and a university researcher might cooperate, for example, to study a problem that the teacher is experiencing in her classroom. The two of them, along with the teachers and educators who read and discuss their research, form a learning community (at least temporarily) for the purpose of sharing the results. Or another example: two teachers might publish the results of jointly exploring why their team-taught classroom has succeeded. By working together and by sharing their experiences with others through publication, the two teachers form part of a "community" of learners, enriching each other's thinking as a result. Or a third example: a school staff plans an individual educational plan cooperatively. Arranging convenient meeting times is difficult for them, but this fact does not prevent collaboration. Or a final example: a seventh-grade teacher and a special education resource teacher try teaching together as a team for the benefit of students. In doing so they create the beginnings of a community of learners, even if it is not a complete community yet. The teachers encounter challenges in working together but the challenges do not prevent them from making the effort. The two have more to say in support of their teamwork:

SHARON: Sure, working together got to be awkward—a division of labor emerged that we hadn't expected. But I would work with Pat again if I had the chance! Pat was great. It's just that we need to think more carefully ahead of time about who's going to do what, and why. Maybe I shouldn't expect to be the equivalent of a full-fledged resource teacher all at once. Maybe I should focus on just one or two students with special needs at first, and make sure the help I give is really something that I can fit into my day. I still think, though, that teaming can be done. I wish more people would try it for the sake of the students.

PAT: Working in Sharon's class helped me more than I expected. I could see the kids with special needs in their "natural habitats" much better than by visiting just occasionally. Sharon reminded me about how precious a classroom teacher's time can be; Sharon had so many students to pay attention to! Most of them were not officially designated as "special-needs" students, but they were needy anyway. You really have to set priorities if you're a classroom teacher and you take the differences among students seriously.

Of course, Pat and Sharon's way of building a community of learners probably will not fit the circumstances and personalities of every high-quality teacher. But as the examples suggest, there are other ways to define a learning community and to become part of one.

A learning community does not even have to exist face to face to be a "community." Imagine Jerod and Cheryl, a brother and sister who communicate entirely by e-mail from separate colleges a hundred miles apart. Yet they learn from each other—in this case, teaching each other important ideas about the nature of learning at a distance. In that respect, at least, they form the kernel of a learning community. In the same way, some teachers—including yourself—may participate in some communities where many of the individuals never meet in person or do so only rarely. These are the communities of teachers and other educators who share professional interests, for example, but live in different cities and meet only occasionally at conferences or professional development days. They are also the "virtual" communities of teachers and educators who share interests or questions but communicate as Jerod and Cheryl do, strictly by electronic correspondence. In spite of seeing one another rarely, these groups also meet the test of a professional community: they provide individuals with support, information, and advice on matters of common interest.

Your Resources for Becoming an Accomplished Teacher

BECOMING an accomplished teacher is indeed challenging, but keep in mind the resources you already have to meet the challenge. Put briefly, there are two: your experiences and your interpretations of experiences. Your experiences give you a basis for caring about students and about education in general, as well as knowledge of particular ways teaching and learning might occur. The interpretations you make of your experiences give you a basis for evaluating experiences and for considering alternatives to them that may be appropriate or desirable.

Your Experiences, Past and Present

No matter what particular experiences you have had with children, classrooms, and teachers, those experiences are a major source of strength in becoming an accomplished teacher, because they are the only place to start developing your own commitments and skills related to teaching. This idea was discussed in Chapter 1, but it is important enough to bear repeating here. Your experiences in schools (and elsewhere) do matter to your development as a teacher, whether they were

A major resource in becoming more professional are your own past experiences and memories about teaching and learning—provided that you supplement these with new experiences and ideas from other professionals.
© Elizabeth Crews

positive or negative, and whether they involved actions and people you admired or ones you would like to escape from. All of your experiences provide building blocks for your development as a teacher, even if they are fragmented and even if you have interpreted them differently now than at the times they occurred. Take these memories and experiences, all from teachers in their first or second year of teaching:

DENIS ENBERG, second grade: You know what I remember most about kindergarten? Watching the tomato plants grow. My parents said the teacher was concerned about that. Even my parents worried. But I just remember enjoying checking them every day, up close, carefully.

SANDRA WATSON, tenth-grade biology: She [my fifth-grade teacher] took us on a field trip to the park. It seemed like the deepest, darkest woods! I loved it; we all did. The teacher seemed more like a human being that day, less like an official "teacher."

TOM SABOURIN, ninth-grade English: The trouble was, he [my seventh-grade social studies teacher] used to single out one or two students and criticize them mercilessly. I still squirm thinking about it! I never want to teach like that, ever.

MARIA TOEWS, sixth grade: We always felt safe there [in my eighth-grade math class]. Mr. Morgan made everyone feel appreciated—even the girls—in spite of obnoxious remarks from a couple of the boys. That mattered to me, even if I never learned eighth-grade math very well.

For all four teachers, past experience provides a starting point for current thinking about their teaching and their students' learning. This is true even for Tom, who criticizes his experience and vows to avoid it in the future; his beliefs and priorities about teaching might be framed differently if he had never witnessed the teacher who he believed "picked on" students. Denis's and Sandra's experiences offer clues about how to teach particular subjects; Maria's and Tom's offer clues about managing and monitoring students. As we will see shortly, none of the four should *end* thinking about teaching and learning with memories of past experiences—nor should you. But everyone begins there, because there is no place else to start.

Memories of personal experiences need not come from the distant past to be relevant. Teachers begin accumulating new ones as soon as they begin teaching, as these three teachers have done:

SHAWNA BUORS, third grade: I'm a lot more comfortable, now that I've tried it, about having a child with special needs in my room. Jill [my student with special needs] was partially sighted, and it didn't really take much adjustment to accommodate her. Some of the kids like to help when she can't read something; in fact, sometimes I have to keep them from helping Jill *too* much.

EMILY MAURO, senior high human ecology: When I found out how the other teacher [of human ecology] prepares for the tests, it sounded great! She has each student write a version of the test; then has a classmate "take" the test by looking for errors in it; then has the two students discuss the results together. I'm going to try it next term.

DAVID VIS, seventh-grade Spanish: I borrowed an idea from a primary teacher at my school, which was to ask students to create their own personal vocabulary lists. Only she [the other teacher] was doing it in English for early readers, and I'm doing it for "early" Spanish speakers, even though they're in seventh grade. Students' responses to having personal lists was so much better [than before], at least for me! Like day and night compared to before.

Note that in these recent or current memories, two of the teachers (Emily and David) have added a new criterion for what makes experience "relevant." Their comments now imply that teaching includes not only classroom events and activities in the presence of students but also planning and collaboration behind the scenes. Otherwise Emily and David would not have commented on an activity that occurs outside class time, the borrowing of ideas from other teachers. In this way, these two teachers show signs of beginning to think systematically about their practice (Proposition 4 in Table 4.1) and beginning to participate in communities of teachers as learners (Proposition 5 in Table 4.1). They also show signs of drawing on the other major resource available to all teachers: their ability to reflect on their work and thereby extend or transform past experiences.

Your Interpretations of Experience

As helpful as personal experiences will be in guiding your teaching and developing your perspectives about education, they will not accomplish these benefits automatically, without your deliberate thought or reflection. By themselves, memories of learning or teaching experiences often do not have clear, agreed-on meanings, although sometimes they may seem to because of assumptions you (or others) make about them. Usually experiences must be interpreted to be useful: reflected on, considered, mulled over, pondered, wondered about, and so on.

From Thoughtful Reflections

One way to interpret experiences is simply to ask questions about them yourself and to make decisions about how the experiences relate to other memories of learning or teaching, or what they imply for your current work with students. Take a closer look at the four teachers' memories of past experiences from the previous section, and consider what each teacher might ask himself or herself about each particular memory:

DENIS ENBERG: Denis might ask himself *why* he chose to tell us that he enjoyed watching the tomato plants grow. Is he saying that he thinks all students should get more chances to garden in elementary school, and perhaps that he is going to provide the chances with his own second-grade class? Or is he saying that children should be allowed to do quiet activities ("just watching") in class without being prodded by the teacher to be more outgoing or active? Or that teachers—perhaps including himself—should be on the lookout for shy children, such as the ones who "just enjoy watching the tomato plants grow," to draw these children out into the social mainstream?

SANDRA WATSON: Sandra might ask herself what she means by saying that on the field trip, the teacher seemed "like a human being." Are teachers not normally human? She might also think about whether "being human" is necessarily good for all kinds of learning, as she implied it was for the field trip. Would it create difficulties in certain situations, such as when a teacher needs emotional distance to help settle a conflict between students or to assess students' work fairly?

MARIA TOEWS: Maria hints that gender bias is an issue for her and that her eighth-grade math teacher was good because somehow he avoided that bias. Maria might need to consider, though, what she admired about *how* the teacher avoided bias. Was it because he responded in a totally "gender-blind" manner to all students, as if he were not even aware of students' gender? Or was it because he deliberately tried to compensate for girls' unfavored status by explicitly inviting them to participate more?

TOM SABOURIN: Tom implies that his seventh-grade social studies teacher was habitually insensitive to students' feelings. Let's assume for the moment that Tom's diagnosis is accurate (although that assumption probably also deserves a closer look). Tom might consider why a teacher might behave in such an inhumane way, or at any rate would give the impression of doing so to students. Are there some clues in the rest of the teacher's behavior that Tom should be aware of to avoid making the same mistake himself, the mistake of accidentally "picking on" students?

From Dialogue with Colleagues

The four teachers—Denis, Sandra, Maria, and Tom—do not have to confine their reflections to themselves. They can, and in fact should, also engage others in the questions they ask. Many ways to do so are accessible to teachers, regardless of level of expertise or experience. The simplest way to engage others is just to *converse* with fellow teachers: What do *you* think of this experience I have had? What do *you* think I should make of it? But more complex ways to involve others are also not difficult to find. *Group study*, for example, occurs frequently in schools as a result of committee work a school needs; teachers gather for the purpose of bringing themselves up to date on a new piece of curriculum, for example, or planning activities related to a schoolwide theme (e.g., "ecology"). The meetings associated with study groups often lead to considerable dialogue about issues of teaching and learning, including the sharing of experiences by other teachers and of their interpretations of them. For a beginning teacher, study groups are a particularly good way to meet experienced, veteran teachers and to learn from them.

Somewhat more formal in organization are professional in-service programs sponsored by a school or school district. Usually these focus on specific areas of current educational concern in the local schools (for example, implementing a new system for managing conflict). They often meet after school or in the evening, and occasionally on half- or whole-days when teachers are released from normal teaching duties. They offer

In Your Own Voice

This discussion leaves out another way to involve colleagues in reflecting on questions of teaching and learning: discussion groups on the Internet.

For suggestions about where to locate some of these, see the Internet Resources section at the end of each chapter.

How would a discussion via e-mail compare, in terms of helpfulness, to the alternatives: (1) no discussion at all or (2) a face-to-face discussion?

a convenient way to converse with colleages, especially those from neighboring schools, and especially if you are indeed concerned about the topic of the in-service program.

Still more formal in organization are graduate courses at a local university. These typically focus on broad topics, issues, or curriculum areas in education, and often provide leads to pursue new reading or educational research—including teacher-designed research—that is interesting and important to teachers. Like in-service programs, graduate courses provide another place to meet and talk with fellow teachers, but courses are more likely to include colleagues not only from your own school district but from others as well, or even from other cities. Many (though not all) of the courses offer opportunities to share and interpret personal experiences related to teaching and learning. Gaining admission to university courses in education generally is not difficult for teachers, although sometimes the courses require a minimum average grade level or minimum amount of classroom experience (one or two years). And, of course, they have tuition costs.

Becoming Truly Professional

As these comments suggest, becoming truly professional is a lifelong challenge—a journey that most teachers begin even before they meet their first classrooms and that takes them places that may be hard to foresee at first. Professionalism is a process more than an outcome—a way of encountering new students and new classroom problems and of finding meaning and solutions to them as you grow. It is not a "thing" acquired and worn like a piece of clothing; at no time will you have become professional once and for all.

While describing professionalism in these terms can make it seem daunting, keep in mind that you are already partly professional because of experiences and goals that you already have. The second section of this chapter showed why this may be so. Chances are that you have already interacted or worked with young people—or at least *lived* as a child or youth! And chances are that you have reflected on those experiences already and very likely have discussed them with others. What remains is to continue gaining new experience, both in the classroom and elsewhere, and to continue revising and expanding your ideas, reflections, and interpretations of the experiences. Adding to your experience will be a big job—really a lifelong challenge—but it *is* one you have already initiated.

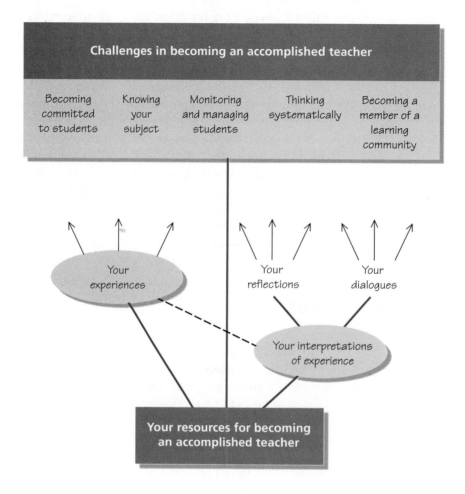

Chapter Re-View: Looking Ahead This Chapter Re-View suggests directions in which the chapter might have taken your thinking—though, of course, other directions are also possible. It expands the Chapter View, which suggests a starting point, conceptually, for the chapter. But this Re-View does not suggest an ending point. Like the Chapter View, it represents just one perspective among many.

Key Terms and Concepts

professional teaching standards (78)

commitment to students (79)

knowing your subject (83)

monitoring and managing students' learning (84)

thinking systematically about practice (86)

learning communities (88)

Annotated Readings

Richardson, Virginia (Ed.). (1997). *Constructivist teaching education: Building a world of new understandings.* London: Falmer Press. Richardson and other educators talk about the challenges of becoming a teacher with a constructivist orientation. Although the authors assume familiarity with constructivism as a point of view about education, they generally write in a very accessible style. In any case, by now you should be becoming familiar with constructivism!

Wasley, P. (1994). *Stirring the chalkdust: Tales of teachers changing classroom practice.* New York: Teachers College Press. The author describes how several teachers undertake new initiatives that make each of them more accomplished educators. Each teacher has unique needs, teaching different subjects, grade levels, and kinds of students; thus each develops in ways that are quite different, yet equally appropriate.

Zemelman, S. (1993). *Best practice: New standards for teaching and learning in America's schools.* Portsmouth, NH: Heinemann. The author describes examples of teachers who explicitly focus on developing skills in the five areas of challenge described in this chapter. On the whole, the teachers succeeded in meeting the challenges—though it was work for them all.

Internet Resources

<www.nbpts.org> This is the web site for the National Board of Professional Teaching Standards. Among other resources, it contains complete explanations of, and justifications for the importance of, the five propositions of accomplished teaching summarized in Table 14.1. It also presents supplementary standards developed by teachers of particular subjects (e.g., mathematics) and grade levels (e.g., early childhood education).

<www.ericsp.org>, <www.yahoo.com/Education/Teaching> Here are two more web sites that emphasize the continuing professional development of teachers. The first is from the ERIC Clearinghouse on Teaching and Teacher Education, a federally funded institute that provides information and support to both new and experienced teachers. Among other things, it includes short, downloadable publications about professional concerns. The second is the site for Yahoo!, a major search engine on the Internet; this particular part of Yahoo! lists various other sites on the Internet that are intended for professional development.

Epilogue: Blurring Distinctions, Enriching Meanings

As I have tried to show in these four chapters, becoming more professional requires your active effort. No one can do it for you. Being professional means gaining experience, of course, but it also means reflecting on the significance of experiences. Reflection creates a framework that informs or gives value to your experiences, which in turn test and stimulate further growth in your thinking—all of which is work, though of a challenging and satisfying kind.

In doing the work of reflection, you may find that traditional educational categories sometimes combine in unexpected ways and blur distinctions you have previously taken for granted. In this primer, for example, the term *teaching* overlaps with both *learning* and *research*. Teaching and learning overlap because teachers are sometimes learners, and learners sometimes teach one another. Teaching means learning both how students think in general and how they think about specific ideas or skills. Learning means knowing how to teach something to others.

But teaching also overlaps with research because certain forms of educational research—in particular, teacher research—actually resemble classroom teaching. Teacher research grows from questions and issues created by classroom teachers in everyday teaching. Yet since everyday teaching can involve systematic reflection, observation, and sharing of results, "teaching" itself resembles "research."

The blurring of traditional distinctions such as these can cloud our understanding of teaching and learning, but it also reflects the richness of the key ideas in education (Davis & Sumara, 1997). *Teaching*, *learning*, and the other major ideas discussed in this primer are indeed complex, full of multiple meanings, and laced with connections between and among each other. They therefore deserve careful, conscious reflection by anyone who plans to use them. As I have tried to show, there are many ways to accomplish such reflection, to ask good questions about teaching and learning. To the extent that you can do so, you and your students will learn more—though perhaps not always in the ways you first expect. The African American writer James Baldwin (1961) said it well, although at the time he was reflecting on how he came to terms with being an African American. When you reflect deeply on your experiences, he said,

The questions which you ask yourself begin . . . to illuminate the world, and become a key to the experience of others.

GLOSSARY

arts-based research a method of research study that takes advantage of an artistic medium in order to heighten readers' understanding of and response to research findings.

constructivism the belief that knowledge is created or "constructed" by individuals' active efforts to make meaning through interactions with other people and with things.

creative thinking generating ideas that are genuinely new, as well as useful and pleasing.

dialogue the active sharing of views intended to clarify differences and identify common ground; dialogue can be internal, thoughtful considerations of ideas and external conversations about them.

educated guesswork a form of trial-and-error behavior based on experience and knowledge of a problem rather than on completely random responses.

education research the systematic study of issues or problems of teaching and learning.

learning a lasting change in behavior or thinking as a result of experience or reflection; learning occurs in all settings, of which classrooms and schools are but two.

learning community a group (actual or virtual) of teachers, parents, and students that fosters collaboration and mutual support in the educational endeavor.

problem solving the analysis and solution of situations that pose difficulties, inconsistencies, or obstacles of some kind.

professional teaching standards the set of qualities and complex skills needed for excellence in teaching; long-term challenging goals for teachers.

reflection the internal, highly individualized act of interpreting experience to draw conclusions or pose further questions.

teaching what teachers do to assist students in learning, both outside of class and inside.

teacher research the sustained, systematic inquiry into the issues and problems one faces as a teacher; in contrast to formal education research, the teacher him- or herself defines the problem being researched. Also called **classroom research.**

thinking the process of forming ideas—a combination of problem solving, creativity, and scholastic aptitude.

transfer the application of knowledge acquired in one situation to another, related situation.

REFERENCES

Amsel, E., Langer, R., & Loutzenhiser, L. (1991). Do lawyers reason differently from psychologists? A comparative design for studying expertise. In R. Sternberg & P. Frensch (Eds.), *Complex problem solving* (pp. 223–252). Hillsdale, NJ: Erlbaum.

Baldwin, J. (1961). *Nobody knows my name: More notes of a native son.* New York: Dial Press.

Barone, T., & Eisner, E. (in press). Arts-based educational research. In R. Jaeger (Ed.), *Complementary methods for research in education* (2nd ed.). Washington, DC: American Educational Research Association.

Bereiter, C. (1994). Implications of postmodernism for science, or science as progressive discourse. *Educational Psychologist, 29*(1), 3–12.

Berlak, H. (1993). *Toward a new science of educational testing and assessment.* Albany, NY: State University of New York.

Bruner, J. (1900). *Acts of meaning.* Cambridge, MA: Harvard University Press.

Bullough, R., Knowles, G., & Crow, N. (1992). *Emerging as a teacher.* London: Routledge.

Clifford, P., & Friesen, S. (1993). A curious plan: Managing on the twelfth. *Harvard Educational Review, 63*(3), 339–358.

Cochran-Smith, M., & Lytle, S. (1993). *Inside/outside: Teacher research and knowledge.* New York: Teachers College Press.

Davis, B., & Sumara, D. (1997). Cognition, complexity, and teacher education. *Harvard Educational Review, 67*(1), 105–125.

Denis, D., Griffin, P., & Cole, M. (1990). *The construction zone: Working for cognitive change in school.* New York: Cambridge University Press.

Edwards, N. (1989). *Stand and deliver.* New York: Scholastic.

REFERENCES

Eisner, Elliot. (1991). *The enlightened eye: Qualitative inquiry and the enhancement of educational practice.* New York: Macmillan.

Eisner, Elliot. (1996, May). *Qualitative research in music education: Past, present, perils, and promise.* Paper presented at the Music Education Research Conference, University of Illinois, Urbana, IL.

Feldman, D. (1986). *Nature's gambit: Child prodigies and the development of human potential.* New York: Basic Books.

Feldman, D. (1988). Creativity: dreams, insights, and transformations. In R. Sternberg (Ed.), *The nature of creativity* (pp. 271–297). New York: Cambridge University Press.

Fenstermacher, G. (1994). The knower and the known: The nature of knowledge in research on teaching. In L. Darling-Hammond (Ed.), *Review of Research in Education* (Vol. 20, pp. 3–56). Washington, DC: American Educational Research Association.

Floden, R., & Buchmann, M. (1990). Philosophical inquiry in teacher education. In W.R. Huston, M. Haberman & J. Sikula (Eds.), *Handbook of research on teacher education* (pp. 42–58). New York: Macmillan

Frederikson, N., Mislevy, R., & Bejar, I. (Eds.). (1993). *Test theory for a new generation of tests.* Hillsdale, NJ: Erlbaum.

Gardner, H. (1993). *Multiple intelligences: The theory in practice.* New York: Basic Books.

Gardner, H. (1994). *Creating minds: An anatomy of creativity seen through the lives of Freud, Einstein, Picasso, Stravinsky, Eliot, Graham, and Gandhi.* New York: Basic Books.

Groen, G., & Patel, V. (1988). The relation between comprehension and reasoning in medical diagnosis. In M. Chi, R. Glaser & M. Farr (Eds.), The nature of expertise (pp. 287–310). Hillsdale, NJ: Erlbaum.

Haney, W. (1993). *The fractured marketplace for standardized tests.* Boston: Kluwer-Nijhoff.

Herrnstein, R., & Murray, C. (1994). *The bell curve: Intelligence and class structure in American life.* New York: Free Press.

Hittleman, D., & Simon, A. (1997). *Interpreting educational research* (2nd ed.). Englewood Cliffs, NJ: Prentice-Hall.

Horn, J. (1989). Models of intelligence. In R. Linn (Ed.), *Intelligence: Measurement, theory, and public policy* (pp. 29–73). Urbana/Champaign, IL: University of Illinois Press.

Hubbard, R., & Power, B. (1993). *The art of classroom inquiry: A handbook for teacher-researchers.* Portsmouth, NH: Heinemann.

Hunt, E. (1991). Some comments on the study of complexity. In R.

Sternberg & P. Frensch (Eds.), *Complex problem solving* (pp. 383–396). Hillsdale, NJ: Erlbaum.

Jones, V. (1998). *Comprehensive classroom management: Creating communities of support and solving problems.* Boston: Allyn and Bacon.

Kamii, C. (Ed.). (1990). *Achievement testing in the early grades: Games grown-ups play.* Washington, DC: National Association for the Education of Young Children.

Kant, I. (1959). *Foundations of the metaphysics of morals.* New York: Liberal Arts Press. (Originally published 1785).

King, P., & K. Kitchener. (1994). *Developing reflective judgment: Understanding and promoting intellectual growth and critical thinking in adolescents and adults.* San Francisco: Jossey-Bass.

Kohn, A. (1996). *Beyond discipline: From compliance to community.* Alexandria, VA: Association for Supervision and Curriculum Development.

Lesgold, A. (1988). Problem solving. In R. Sternberg & E. Smith (Eds.), *The psychology of human thought* (pp. 188–213). New York: Cambridge University Press.

Lesgold, A., Rubinson, H., Feltovich, P., Glaser, R., Klopfer, D., & Wang, Y. (1988). Expertise in a complex skill: Diagnosing X-ray pictures. In M. Chi, R. Glaser & M. Farr (Eds.), *The nature of expertise* (pp. 311–342). Hillsdale, NJ: Erlbaum.

National Board for Professional Teaching Standards. (1997). *What teachers should know and be able to do* [online]. Available at <www.nbpts.org/nbpts/standards/intro.html>.

Norris, S. (1992). *Generalizability of critical thinking: Multiple perspectives on an educational ideal.* New York: Teachers College Press.

Nye, N., Delclose, V., Burns, M., & Bransford, J. (1988). Teaching thinking and problem solving. In R. Sternberg & E. Smith (Eds.), *The psychology of human thought* (pp. 337–365). New York: Cambridge University Press.

Overton, W. (1991). The structure of developmental theory. In H. W. Reese (Ed.), *Advances in child development and behavior* (pp. 1–37). San Diego: Academic Press.

Paley, V. (1986). *Mollie is three.* Chicago: University of Chicago Press.

Partin, R. (1995). *Classroom teachers' survival guide: Strategies, maangement techniques, and reproducibles for new and experienced teachers.* West Nyack, NY: Center for Applied Research in Education.

Perkins, D. (1992). *Smart schools: Better thinking and learning for every child.* New York: Free Press.

Perrone, V. (Ed.). (1991). *Expanding student assessment*. Alexandria, VA: Association for Supervision and Curriculum Development.

Phillips, D. C. (1992). *The social scientist's bestiary: A guide to fabled threats to, and defences of, naturalistic social science*. New York: Permagon Press.

Phillips, D. C. (1994). Telling it straight: Issues in assessing narrative research. *Educational Psychologist, 29*(1), 13–22.

Piaget, J. (1965). *The moral judgment of the child*. New York: Free Press. (Originally published 1932).

Resnick, L. (1987). Learning in school and out. *Educational Researcher, 16*(9), 13–20.

Resnick, L., Levine, J., & Teasley, S. (1991). *Perspectives on social shared cognition*. Washington, DC: American Psychological Association.

Richardson, V. (1994). Conducting research on practice. *Educational Researcher, 23*(5), 5–10.

Russell, T., & Munby, H. (1991). Reframing: The role of experience in developing teachers' professional knowledge. In D. A. Schön (Ed.), *The reflective turn* (pp. 164–187). New York: Teachers College Press.

Schön, D. (Ed.). (1991). *The reflective turn*. New York: Teachers College Press.

Seifert, K. (1992). What develops in informal theories of development? *Journal of Learning about Learning, 5*(1), 4–11.

Seifert, K., & Handziuk, D. (1993, March). *Ontological commitments to the child*. Paper presented at the biennial meeting of the Society for Research on Child Development, New Orleans.

Sizer, Theodore. (1996). *Horace's hope: What works for American high schools*. Boston: Houghton Mifflin.

Sosniak, L. (1990). The tortoise, the hare, and the development of talent. In M. Howe (Ed.), *Encouraging the development of exceptional skills and talents* (pp. 149–164). Leicester, UK: British Psychological Society.

Stenhouse, L. (1985). *Research as a basis for teaching*. London: Heinemann.

Sternberg, R. (1990). *Metaphors of mind: Conceptions of the nature of intelligence*. Cambridge: Cambridge University Press.

Sternberg, R., & Frensch, P. (1991). *Complex problem solving*. Hillsdale, NJ: Erlbaum.

Strange, J. (1997). *Evaluating teachers: A guide to current thinking and best practice*. Thousand Oaks, CA: Corwin Press.

Task Force on Teaching as a Profession. (1986). *A nation prepared*. Washington, DC: The Forum.

Thorndike, R., Hagen, E., & Sattler, J. (1986). *Stanford-Binet Intelligence Scale* (4th ed.). Chicago: Riverside Publishing.

Tucke-Bressler, M. (1992). Giftedness, creativity, and productive thinking: Towards a unification of theoretical concepts and empirical research. In J. Carlson (Ed.), *Cognition and educational practice* (Vol. 2, pp. 131–149). Greenwich, CT: JAI Press.

Twain, M. (1899). *Pudd'nhead Wilson.* New York: Harper, 1899.

Ulnichy, P., & Schoener, W. (1996). Teacher-researcher collaboration from two perspectives. *Harvard Educational Review, 66*(3), 496–524.

Wagner, R. (1991). Managerial problem solving. In R. Sternberg & P. Frensch (Eds.), *Complex problem solving* (pp. 159–182). Hillsdale, NJ: Erlbaum.

Wallace, D., & Gruber, H. (Eds.). (1992). *Creative people at work: Twelve cognitive case studies.* New York: Oxford University Press.

Wilson, S. (1995). Not tension but intention: A response to Wong's analysis of the researcher/teacher. *Educational Researcher, 24*(8), 19–22.

Wong, E. D. (1995). Challenges confronting the researcher/teacher: Conflicts of purpose and conduct. *Educational Researcher, 24*(3), 22–28.

If you would like to examine this primer's parent text:

Constructing a Psychology of Teaching and Learning
Kelvin Seifert © 1999
(title code: 3-51800   ISBN: 0-395-70808-7)

---

please call our Faculty Service Center at

Houghton Mifflin Company
2075 Foxfield Road, Suite 100
St. Charles, IL 60174
1-800-733-1717 FAX 1-800-733-1810
http://www.hmco.com/college

Brief Table of Contents for
Constructing a Psychology of Teaching and Learning: